T0328342

"This brilliant and pioneering book, filled with erudition and passion, is the fruit of decades of exploring the relationship between myth and politics through the medium of the psyche. And not just the personal psyche, but also the collective psyche we share as members of our own particular culture and, further, the archetypal psyche that we all inherit as members of the human race—expressed in myth and dreams and our instinctive responses to the world. As Tom Singer puts it: 'perhaps one of the greatest prerogatives of being human is the right to take up unanswerable questions, posed by the facts of our lives.' Singer pursues these questions by summoning the different voices of the psyche—distinguishing, for instance, the cultural complex from the personal complex, so both may be more clearly heard. The aim—luminously achieved in this book—is that life may be lived with more understanding and compassion and, of course, with more joy and laughter."

—*Jules Cashford, England, mythologist and Jungian analyst*

"C. G. Jung was an introverted religious man, a *homo religiosus*, but as a *homo politicus* he was not so successful in his time. However, his groundbreaking ideas about the Self and the collective unconscious in relation to the psyche of the group, as further developed here by Thomas Singer, provide insight into the turmoil of our times. Especially useful is the concept of the cultural complex in helping decipher the cultural and political world of today, particularly after the collapse of the Eastern Block, and in the psychological earthquakes of our current ecological crisis. This book is a must for anyone who wants to see deeper than what is visible in the daily news."

—*Joerg Rasche, Berlin, Jungian analyst, honored with the Golden Cross of Merit by the President of Poland for his work in reconciling the peoples of Europe*

"Dr. Thomas Singer is among a handful of psychiatrists who widen the focus of the psychic eye. His writings place the distressed person into the cauldron of the greater communal stress. Because Dr. Singer is an honest American, he lets you track him working through the puzzle of his nation— of his own self in that nation and his place in it as a doctor of souls. Singer's humility and vision throw light on forces shaping conflict and shaping the United States. The Great Unconscious America maddens people. Can anyone turn on the lights? What is the cure? Can there be a cure to folly? For the truth is, this is the Age of Folly, playing out from the steps of the White House to the ends of the world. Singer's book analyzes this maddening thing: this folly—this Age of Anxiety. Attend to him."

—*Craig San Roque, Sydney, Australia, analytical psychologist*

Vision, Reality and Complex

Vision, Reality and Complex brings together a rich selection of Thomas Singer's scholarship on the development of the cultural complex theory and explores the relationship between vision, reality, and illusion in politics and psyche.

The chapters in this book discuss the basic principles of the cultural complex theory in various national and international contexts that span the Clinton, Bush, Obama, and Trump eras. Each chapter grounds this theory in practical examples, such as race and health care in the United States, or in specific historical and international conflicts between groups, whether they be ethnic, racial, gender, local, national, or global. With chapters on topics including mythology, leadership, individuation, revolution, war, and the soul, Singer's work provides unique insights into contemporary culture, activism, and politics.

This collection of essays demonstrates how the cultural complex theory applies in specific contexts while simultaneously having cross-cultural relevance through the reemergence of complexes throughout history. It is essential reading for academics and students of Jungian and post-Jungian ideas, politics, sociology, and international studies, as well as for practicing and trainee analysts alike.

Thomas Singer, MD, is a psychiatrist and Jungian psychoanalyst who trained at Yale Medical School, Dartmouth Medical School, and the C. G. Jung Institute of San Francisco. He is the author of many books and articles that include a series of books on cultural complexes that have focused on Australia, Latin America, Europe, the United States, and Far East Asian countries, in addition to another series of books featuring Ancient Greece, Modern Psyche. He serves on the board of ARAS (Archive for Research into Archetypal Symbolism) and has served as coeditor of *ARAS Connections* for many years.

Routledge Focus on Jung, Politics and Culture

The Jung, Politics and Culture series showcases the "political turn" in Jungian and Post-Jungian psychology. Established and emerging authors offer unique perspectives and new insights as they explore the connections between Jungian psychology and key topics—including national and international politics, gender, race and human rights.

For a full list of titles in this series, please visit www.routledge.com/Focus-on-Jung-Politics-and-Culture/book-series/FJPC

Titles in the series:

From Vision to Folly in the American Soul
Jung, Politics and Culture
Thomas Singer

Vision, Reality and Complex
Jung, Politics and Culture
Thomas Singer

Vision, Reality and Complex
Jung, Politics and Culture

Thomas Singer

Routledge
Taylor & Francis Group

LONDON AND NEW YORK

First published 2021
by Routledge
2 Park Square, Milton Park, Abingdon, Oxon OX14 4RN

and by Routledge
52 Vanderbilt Avenue, New York, NY 10017

Routledge is an imprint of the Taylor & Francis Group, an informa business

British Library Cataloguing-in-Publication Data
A catalogue record for this book is available from the British Library

Library of Congress Cataloging-in-Publication Data
Names: Singer, Thomas, 1942– author.
Title: Vision, reality and complex : Jung, politics and culture / Thomas Singer.
Identifiers: LCCN 2020033745 (print) | LCCN 2020033746 (ebook) |
ISBN 9780367538187 (hardback) | ISBN 9780367538132 (paperback) |
ISBN 9781003083399 (ebook)
Subjects: LCSH: Jungian psychology. | Social psychology. | Myth. |
Political culture. | Psychoanalysis and culture.
Classification: LCC BF173.J85 S538 2020 (print) |
LCC BF173.J85 (ebook) | DDC 150.19/54–dc23
LC record available at https://lccn.loc.gov/2020033745
LC ebook record available at https://lccn.loc.gov/2020033746

ISBN: 978-0-367-53818-7 (hbk)
ISBN: 978-1-003-08339-9 (ebk)

Typeset in Times
by Newgen Publishing UK

I dedicate this book to Andrew Samuels with respect, admiration, and love. He has been an inspiration in exploring the boundaries between a psychological attitude and political activism. This book would simply not exist without Andrew's initiative in so many areas, not the least of which is the creation of the Routledge series on Jung, Politics and Culture.

Contents

Figures

Acknowledgments

LeeAnn Pickrell's care in fitting all the pieces of this book together goes way beyond professionalism. She is an artist in her way of knowing how to bring a complicated project to fruition—from the smallest detail to the broadest concept. And she is a joy to work with ...

Introduction

It is a daunting task as well as a great honor to be given the opportunity to make a selection from my papers over time in such a way as to create a new entity—hopefully one that holds together and has its own rhythms and resonances as if it were a single creation in itself. This moment for gathering my reflections seems particularly ripe in terms of the great distress that has engulfed much of the globe (though many authors of other eras have often said the same thing during calamitous times). In the process of selecting the papers, I found that complementary tracks emerged that have resulted in two separate but related books. This first book, *Vision, Reality and Complex: Jung, Politics and Culture,* follows the development of the cultural complex theory. The second, complementary book, *From Vision to Folly in the American Soul: Jung, Politics, and Culture,* focuses more specifically on the American experience, both in terms of personal and collective identity and soul.

So many questions have accompanied the gathering together of these papers. Does what I have written make any sense? Is it relevant? Is there a discernable development of themes and depth? Will anyone be interested? Of course, all of this is ultimately for the reader to decide. But undertaking such a task leads to my own wondering: what is it that I have been laboring to express over these several decades? If Jung was right about there being a "spirit of the depths" and a "spirit of the times," I hope that there is enough of a balance between the two in my musings, that there is both a sense of specificity in terms of historic context as well as a sense of depth that allows the reader to see connections over and through time, even with glimpses into the timeless.

A major theme of this book is an inquiry into the relationships between politics, psyche, and mythology. This theme first emerges in the opening chapter: "Introduction to the Vision Thing," which I wrote in 2000. That inquiry began to take more specific shape in the early years of the twenty-first century as the cultural complex theory developed. Many of the chapterss in this book reflect my effort to work out the basic principles of this theory in various national and international contexts. I have always tried to ground the theory in practical examples such as race and healthcare in the United States or in specific historical and international conflicts between groups, whether they be ethnic, racial, gender, local, national, or global. In addition to my own essays on the cultural complex theory, I have sought to test the hypothesis in the past decades by editing six books on the topic with some ninety different authors making contributions from Australia, Latin America, Europe, North America, and Far East Asia. The goal of the series has been to tease out how the cultural complex theory applies in specific contexts while simultaneously having cross-cultural relevance.

This volume documents my exploration of the cultural complex theory as I have wondered about how psyche, politics, and mythology get so mired in our minds, hearts, and spirits. Perhaps the final chapter of this book is fittingly placed as it takes this exploration to the edge of the precipice in the emergence of extinction anxiety as a contemporary global phenomenon, reflecting the age-old crucible of psyche, politics, and culture in the difficult effort to tease out what is vision, what is reality, and what is complex.

Dear readers

Because there is a limitation on the number of images that can be included in a print text, I have created a special arrangement with ARAS (the Archive for Research in Archetypal Symbolism) that permits me to link the reader to more images that add greatly to the written text. ARAS has graciously set up a special place on their website for readers to access these images, which can be reached simply by typing on a computer the URL link indicated at the appropriate places in the text: **https://aras.org/vision-reality-complex**. Once readers arrive at the ARAS file hosting this feature, they will be able to view the specific image according to chapter location.

1   Introduction to *The Vision Thing*

From *The Vision Thing: Myth, Politics and Psyche in the World*, edited by Thomas Singer, Routledge, 2000.[1]

This chapter served as the introduction to The Vision Thing: Myth, Politics and Psyche *in the World, a collection of essays that originated during a small conference over a stormy weekend at the funky Bolinas Rod & Boat Club in 1999. Featuring Jungian analysts and politicians, the conference began with a conversation I had in 1989 with Senator Bill Bradley who, along with many others as the turn of the millennium approached, wondered "What Myth Now?" I did not know it at the time, but it was the beginning of my decades-long circumambulation around the interfaces of myth, politics, and psyche in the world.*

There are times when politicians stumble into the need to link the political and mythological. They are propelled by a peculiar mix of dire necessity, conscious intention, and a deep unconscious sense of collective need. The title of this book is taken from a phrase born out of just such a situation. Although George H. W. Bush had recently "won" the Gulf War and conventional wisdom had it that he was unbeatable in 1992, the president was having trouble communicating with the American people—especially around domestic policy, as so poignantly revealed when he went shopping at a supermarket and didn't know what a bar code was at the check-out counter. The president had lost touch with everyday life and people in his own country. His reelection campaign began to implode. Bush himself identified part of his problem connecting with a restless electorate as "The Vision Thing."

   The Vision Thing—a phrase that Bush had inadvertently coined early in his administration as a self-acknowledged problem of articulating a clear vision—had been haunting him for four years. He often joked about it in his speeches in an attempt to defuse the implicit criticism that, in fact, he had little or no intuition as to where the country was or ought to be headed. In a futile attempt to resurrect his lame 1992 campaign, Bush tried to fill the vision gap by referring to a past "vision" of the sunrise of American promise he had when he was plucked from the Pacific as a downed fighter pilot in World War II, just as in 1988, in his inaugural address, he had sentimentally kindled a future vision "to make kinder the face of the nation and gentler the face of the world" nursed by "a thousand points of light."

Although Bush failed to fill the vision gap in the 1992 election, he did leave us to ponder his legacy of "The Vision Thing." This book's title was chosen from his aptly awkward attempt to link political reality with archetypal vision—not to mock George Bush, but to acknowledge the awesome difficulty of uniting vision with reality. In truth, "The Vision Thing" experienced at a personal and collective level attempts to bring together the political and mythological realms through psychological experience. "Vision" is seen with the mind's or spirit's eye, and "thing" designates the most basic, concrete stuff of reality. "Vision" and "thing" do not fit comfortably together. It is the rare leader who can put "vision" and "thing" together in a believable way; it is the rare leader who can articulate a true vision that fits with real politics.

Origin of idea

The idea for this "vision thing" book grew out of a conversation I had with Senator Bill Bradley in 1989. Over dinner one night Senator Bradley asked about Joseph Campbell's life-long study of mythology. Public interest in Campbell was peaking at the time, and Senator Bradley was curious both about Campbell's work itself and the increasing public attention given to mythological themes. He wanted to understand more about the importance of myth in human affairs and, specifically, what was currently capturing the public imagination about the study and insights of mythology. Our talk was not about myth in its popular use as "inaccurate fiction" but about how in some mysterious way a living myth establishes a meaningful link between humans, nature, and spirit. In this use of the word *myth* is the central story a people tells about itself to understand its beginnings, its purposes, and its place in a broader historical and cosmic order. At the heart of Senator Bradley's inquiry were the pragmatic American political questions: "What myth, now? What stories are people telling about themselves and our world now?"

Initial dream

The conversation with Senator Bradley stirred me deeply, and that night I had what C. G. Jung called a "big dream." It seemed to be a comment on the relationship between collective consciousness, as expressed in political reality, and collective unconsciousness, as expressed in myth, vision, and dream. I will offer the heart of the dream, though a "private" communication, because I believe that if we are serious about engaging what lies beneath the surface of our individual and collective lives, it is best to begin at home and because my home-made vision became a kind of guide, question, warning, and meditation that I kept very much in mind as the themes of this book (and all my future studies of vision and folly) unfolded (over decades). Here is my dream's central section: *I am talking to an ancient sage about the meaning of the rapid changes taking place in the world as the millennium approaches. He has his hands on the skull of a black monastic nun from the early Christian era.* The puzzling dream, with its hints of an unfamiliar past political history, teased me with its elusive profundity. Over the years of gathering the pieces of *The Vision Thing,* it constantly reminded me that the questions the authors of this book are asking are huge, not easily answered, and require a creative imagination that can embrace the profound changes in our political, economic, geographic, and even cosmological reality. The dream reminded me that such upheavals also marked the early Christian era and to my Jungian ears suggests a mystery surrounding something dark, feminine, spiritual, and long removed from the world. With the advent of the millennium many prophets are coming forth with crystal ball prophecies of what is in store for our civilization and planet. They shout at us with enormous conviction on the truth of their ready-made intuitions and fill our heads with Utopian promises that are either technological or anti-technological. Black and white, boom or bust prophecies, and strangely empty metaphors about our "need to prepare for the twenty-first century" suggest a poverty of ideas as we grapple with the awesomeness of a truly unknown and unenvisioned future.

One California Jungian analyst's meditation on the skull of a black nun from the early Christian era does not provide any better crystal ball. Rather, such a meditation assures us only of the certainty of death; underlines the turmoil and upheaval of a world in rapid transition; and behind it all evokes the eternal presence of religious mystery. The image, moreover, moves beyond a Christian, Western perspective on these matters. Like a Tibetan monk contemplating a skull in daily religious practice, my "sage" seems to suggest that we can look upon the skull both in the horror of human destruction and as a reminder that death is always our companion in life. As Hamlet knew, our individual lives will soon end in death, and the life of our times will shortly be but a skull in the hands of future generations. Our times are fleeting. Do they matter at all? How can we make them count?

Negative capability

Thankfully, my solution has not been to rededicate myself with firmer twentieth-century resolve to the pursuit of a unitary saving vision. Rather, in the spirit of the dream, this book seeks to cultivate the art of not knowing. It is the same art that Keats urged for the poet—what he called "the negative capability," by which he meant the deepest receptivity, free from any overriding insistence on a particular point of view.[2] This attitude is quite different from that taken by those who address us with their daily, instant interpretations of political and cultural life. Reality becomes a toy in their hands in which the meaning of events appears to precede the actual unfolding of the events themselves. Perhaps this is the shadow side of our so-called information technology. The more information we get, the less we really know. It is small wonder that skeptical deconstruction has become the dominant philosophical stance of our times. Retreat into an absurdist position of refusing to ascribe meaning to anything seems like the only reasonable way to escape the tyranny of spin doctors' instant analysis. Perhaps more useful in the long run will not be the refusal to give a definite meaning to anything, but the hard effort of holding open the door to meaning in the hope that it may reveal itself in time. Without that, we are stuck with accepting instantaneous meaning or its opposite, across-the-board meaninglessness. "Negative capability" as receptivity urges holding open the space of not knowing long enough for something authentic to emerge. When we pursue an inquiry about our collective mythological, psychological, and political future, it is an attitude worth cultivating.

The common observation of those who study myth and history is that it is almost impossible to know the myth or myths of the times one is living through. If this is true, why should we even bother to ask the basic question of this book, "What myth(s) now?" One answer is, because the question has already posed itself to us. Perhaps one of the greatest prerogatives of being human is the right to take up unanswerable questions posed by the facts of our lives. For example, many of us who came of age in the 1960s shared an almost tribal assumption that we were participating in the birth of a new era and that we had even glimpsed the outlines of its universal mythology. How different that time and even the myths we thought we were giving birth to appear now through the rather short lens of a few decades! Very few people of my generation know more than that they aren't in Kansas anymore. So the idea behind this book which began with a straightforward question from a thoughtful politician—"What myth now?"—can also be phrased, "Where are we now?" This is the kind of question that can only be answered through dialogue. The actual work on this book began when the politician's reasonable question engaged the nonrational dream response of a psychiatrist trained to read such compensatory, unconscious communications in the tradition of Jungian analytical psychology. This first exchange between two very different kinds of mindset establishes the basic paradoxes and tensions the book sets out to explore: conscious and unconscious, politics and myth, reality and vision—all mediated by the psychology of individuals sharing and trying to envision the same collective psyche.

Myth, politics, psyche

The basic assumption of the book is that there are deep, highly charged, unexplored relationships between mythological or archetypal reality, psychological reality, and political reality. I have sometimes pictured this as a continuum:

myth/archetype ⟷ psyche ⟷ politics

On one end of the spectrum is the purely mythological or archetypal realm with its grand themes of death and rebirth, inner transformation and outer renewal, human and God. On the other end of the imaginary spectrum is the realm of everyday politics with its power plays, deals, persona appearances and deceptions, and a quite substantial knowledge of the practical world. Politicians are at least as adept at shrewdly engaging the reality of the "shadow" as analytical psychologists—even if they do not use the same jargon. In the model I am proposing, psyche sits between and mediates the exchange between myth and politics. Individual fears, aspirations, and conflicts are part of this psyche. Psyche also has a collective aspect that carries the conscious and unconscious concerns and values of the group in which the individual lives. It is the tension and interaction between myth, psyche, and politics in the world that this book proposes to explore. In a way, there is nothing new about this exploration. The Upanishads, the Koran, the Bible, and just about every other sacred scripture of the world's great religions wrestle continuously with the theme of man as a political animal against the backdrop of deep archetypal encounters with spirit.

So the questions addressed by this book are at once old, timeless, and contemporary. Perhaps what makes its way of exploring them new is the psychological effort to make a bit more conscious the nature of the tension and interaction between mythological and political realities. Intuition tells us that such relationships are everywhere, nowhere more pronounced than in our culture's media intermingling of myth, politics, and entertainment. The "American dream," for instance, is still a vital myth with deep political resonance. The underlying linkage is self-evident. We hardly question the fact that much of American politics is deliberately dressed up to give the appearance of fulfilling the material and social promises of that "dream." What is not self-evident is the teasing out of the relationship between the mythic "dream" and the actual politics, because most people are not accustomed to think of myth, psychology, and politics at the same time.

But, in my thinking, myth, psychology, and politics are so entwined in the collective psyche—often quite unconsciously—that we might even think of them as bound together in some kind of marriage. Yet, strangely, as with the forces influencing other marriages, we have trouble articulating clearly the relationship between them or even talking about them at the same time. The expedient and practical do not mix easily or naturally with the symbolic and inner. And yet myth does not exist without embodiment in politics, and politics always has deep, unconscious origins in the stories of a people and its leaders.

There is an inherent opposition between the kinds of people who are most interested in the inner dynamic of archetypal reality and those interested in everyday politics, just as there is an inherent tension between mythological thinking and political thinking. Both have different modes of perception, of apprehending the world. They represent different ways of being in the world. Put someone who sees the world archetypally in a room with a politician, and the dialogue quickly dissolves into misunderstanding and confusion. For instance, quite savvy and articulate students of politics and history can go a bit dumb when the conversation turns to the realm of myth and psyche as if these "spacey" ideas have nothing to do with the everyday affairs of men and women. Real discussion quickly breaks down into mutual distrust. Those who are archetypal and psychological in their thinking display disdain for the mundane machinations of the politician, and those who are political in their thinking perceive (quite accurately) that these more rarefied psychologically minded thinkers do not understand how the real world of human deal-making works.

The collective psyche

Another factor in the tangled relationship between myth and politics is the notion of the "collective psyche." At the heart of this book is the idea that the tension between myth and politics is mediated, intensified, and transmitted by a psyche that is somehow shared by all of us and articulated by a psychology that we hold in common. C. G. Jung wrote: "… the human psyche is not a self-contained and wholly individual phenomenon, but also a collective one."[3] The word *psyche* derives from the Greek, meaning "soul," and usually psyche, like soul, is conceived of as an individual phenomenon. It was Jung's discovery that not only is the individual psyche real, but also there is a living "collective psyche" that arises out of the group or "collective" experience of human beings, and that this collective psyche has an objective reality beyond the interpretations accorded it by different individuals. It is important to note that the collective psyche is not just real in groups. The collective psyche is alive and operative in the individual as well as a transpersonal force to be reckoned with. Just as the individual psyche gives expression to the ripples of deep personal yearnings, one can picture the collective psyche as providing the strong currents and tides in the ocean of common human concerns. Like ocean currents, they are often imperceptible, unfathomable, and moving in conflicting directions. Occasionally, however, collective trends coalesce into large and unpredictable waves that dramatically alter the course of human affairs.

An example of such a potent wave moving through the collective psyche and landing differently in different groups of individuals is the contemporary struggle over what kind of leaders we want to have. A good argument is being made that at least a piece of our present crisis in political leadership is about what kind of "father" (or "mother") should lead us at this time: firm or loose, principled or responsive. There are some authorities whose leadership is solidly rooted in principle and order. They are firm, sometimes stern—but always grounding their authority in principle, as befits the father archetype that informs their "patriarchal" behavior. Margaret Thatcher was such a "father." There is another more modern type of "father"/"mother" whose strength is based on a fluid sensitivity to the changing needs of the family and community. Loose and flexible, his or her fatherhood or motherhood is based less on principle than responsiveness. It is fascinating how Republicans like George H. W. and George W. Bush are talking about "compassionate conservatism" and Democrats are trying to show that they are firm on economic matters while still being responsive to social issues. Both parties are trying to find the right balance of firm and loose "fathers," leaders who will be both principled and responsive in their models of leadership. Obviously, the image of leadership in the collective psyche is in flux and it lands in the individual psyche with different resonances depending on the kind of fatherhood (and motherhood) one has had, not had, or yearned for.

There are many people who do not believe in an individual psyche, much less a collective psyche. For them, the individual psyche is a Romantic, and before that neo-Platonic hangover soon to be replaced by the rational Aristotelian coupling of neuropsychology and psychopharmacology. Within such scientized monikers, "psyche" is getting buried in mind's neurology and pharmacology. By scientific rationalists, the idea of a "collective psyche" is often dismissed as mystical nonsense. Those who reject the notions of an individual and collective psyche argue that the attitudes, moods, and values of the population are more accurately explained by the rational social sciences of economics, politics, and sociology, which can be measured and tracked by statistics. "It's the economy, stupid!" is sometimes their knee-jerk explanation for what most affects the electorate. Given the importance of money in our lives, this reduction of political motivation to a material cause makes sense. But not always. The "collective psyche" has a spiritual zeitgeist dimension that is not reducible to sociology or economics. Ask any good advertising executive, stock market analyst, political pollster, or sportscaster what moves large groups of people. They may not call it the "collective psyche" by name, but they will allude to an ineffable, mysterious, powerful, nonrational force with currents that run strong and deep and that, more often than not, behaves like an unpredictable beast from the watery depths. Occasionally the beast displays its own uncanny wisdom, even if more often it behaves with the mindless force of a large group of adolescents bombarded with hormones. Yet it always has an idea or value that seems to be energizing it. Analytical psychologists call this the "collective psyche."

Vision and reality

Another characteristic of the relationship between myth and politics is that a tension between vision and reality seems to be wired into the psyche. This inherent conflict is experienced universally in the individual and in the collective or social order. One can say that it is archetypal in the sense that typically patterned behaviors, images, and deep feelings emerge in response to the activation of the conflict between vision and reality.

In the life of the individual, for example, most of us have an internal image or vision of what is beautiful. I had a view from our house that looked toward a mountain without a single human-made structure visible. When a neighbor built a new road that cut a white cement line right through the heart of that uninterrupted view, not only was the view of the mountain itself altered, but also my inner image of beauty was violated. Such injuries affect one's sense of well-being and lead to some predictably intense emotional reactions. All of us encounter such conflicts between vision and reality every day and throughout our lives—when our vision of what we should be as children or parents collides with what we know to be the reality of our being a child or parent; or when our vision of a "ripe old age" runs up against age's often harsh realities; and even on a daily basis when the fair play that we envision for our roadways is forced to endure the heedless interactions and rude exchanges we, in fact, discover daily on our highways.

If the vision we have of our individual lives is challenged at every phase of development by the reality of our natural abilities and the opportunities available to us, so too the conflict between vision and reality is exponentially amplified in collective and political life. The best and worst politicians appeal to what we envision to be a good society or even a "great society." That visionary appeal to an inner image is almost always undermined by the reality of what is possible and real. How many promises of the visionary are made to us every day through the seductively powerful assault on our collective psyche by images from television, films, the internet, and especially savvy advertisers who have the art of passing off the visionary as sellable reality down to a science? The impact occurs at subliminal levels where we are conditioned to believe in these promises. The inevitable experience of the gap between these visionary promises and the reality we discover expresses itself in frustration and anger, which can lead to either disillusionment and withdrawal or a mobilization to action and the desire "to do something about it." The tension between vision and reality is as wired into the collective psyche as it is to the individual psyche, whether we get our primal stories and images from the village elders of old or the modern transmitters of our shared stories—movies, television, and the internet.

Many politicians make a career out of exploiting the tension between vision and reality by rubbing our faces in the discrepancy between what has been promised in visionary terms and what has been delivered in real terms. Others try to help us see and close the gap by offering viable links between the visionary and the real. Perhaps the best of times is when there is a shared coherent vision of the natural, social, and religious order that provides ongoing meaning to the realities of everyday life—however harsh they may be. (The way the country gathered together to make sure "the system worked" in the Watergate crisis might be an example.) One might say that in those times the inherent tension between vision and reality is creative and that the realities of everyday life neither mock unattainable promises of the visionary nor undermine the vision of the whole. Perhaps the worst of times is when a shared vision of the world is disintegrating and the demands of everyday reality are intolerable. (The riots in Chicago at the time of the 1968 Democratic Convention were an example of this.) And perhaps the most exciting of times is when there are competing visions of the world order and the demands of reality are not so harsh and limited that the freedom to experiment is restricted. We may be in such a time now.

In our so-called post-modern life rarely is there a shared vision in the collective psyche of what would be best for the social order, and often there is profound disagreement even on what is real. When President Clinton of the United States is reduced to defending himself in public with the statement, "It depends on what 'is' means," it might signal that it is no longer safe to place much faith in our conventional sense of reality. "Is" is one of the most basic things we can say about reality. With little shared vision or even consensus on what is real, the gap between vision and reality widens and we are left to the national pastime of carping disbelief. We indulge in visionary expectations and hyperbole (our fantastic celebrities and Super Bowls and Academy Awards) and then delight in the collapse of what we have built up in our collective imagination and what we think reality has delivered us. Beneath this split between vision and reality, it is important to keep in mind that the most enduring myths as embodied in the world's great religions—Hinduism, Buddhism, Muslim, Jewish, and Christian—have always been able to speak to the deepest yearnings, the deepest sufferings, and the deepest joys of large groups of people. The enduring myths are able to bridge the inherent tension between vision and reality. They are able to connect the deepest truths of human vision to the most mundane levels of reality.

Having affirmed (1) the complex intermingling of myth, politics, and psyche, (2) the reality of the collective psyche, and (3) the inherent tension between vision and reality, it is time to give an example from our recent political past of how these forces play themselves out. I have discovered that while many can agree in principle with the notion of the interpenetration of myth, psyche, and politics, it is harder to find a consensus in interpretation when one actually examines a specific case history. Everybody seems to bring their own myth and psyche to controversial political conflicts, which perhaps only further illustrates the powerful interweaving of these forces.

Myth, politics, and psyche in the case of health care reform

Bill Clinton surprised many people when he came out of nowhere to challenge George Bush in the 1992 presidential elections. Clinton's fresh face and new energy was in stark contrast to George Bush's tired inability to articulate a domestic policy and his failure to convincingly address what he himself called "The Vision Thing." Clinton's campaign effort gained substantial momentum as he rode a popular wave of disgust with health insurance companies that coupled with his timely call for national health care reform. It seemed inexcusable to the aroused electorate that close to twenty (or was it thirty?) million employed Americans did not have basic health insurance. The collective psyche was mobilized for real change, and Clinton capitalized on this profound shift in mood to win the election. Emboldened by the mandate for health care reform and the emerging new myth of men and women as truly equal partners in work/leadership as well as marriage, Clinton turned over the day-to-day task of bringing about health care reform to his wife shortly after the election. Together, they vowed to achieve 100 percent universal health care, not 95 percent.

By many accounts, however, the Clintons along with their chief architect of reform, Ira Magaziner, were arrogant, did not listen to their natural allies, and refused to compromise even when they were close to achieving most of their goals. The brief window of opportunity for significant reform slammed shut. The insurance companies, which had been on the defensive, were let off the hook, and they simply redoubled their formidable resistance to any significant reform. The aroused electorate sank back into apathy. The push for reform collapsed without any tangible accomplishments.

To link the colossal failure of Clinton's national health care proposal to the psychic inflation of a relatively young man over-identified with the hero myth takes a little explaining. Clinton wanted to be the dragon slayer. The dragon was clearly the collective power of insurance companies, drug companies, and all of the vastly powerful economic interests that were motivated mainly by the desire to preserve profits, not necessarily to provide quality care for the entire population. Like every hero caught in the grandiose self-idealization of an archetypal inflation, Clinton promised and believed that he could slay the dragon and deliver a boon to his suffering nation—in this case, the heroic accomplishment of freeing up health care from the clutches of entrenched financial interests and delivering it to a "universal" population. This was the vision that filled many Americans with new hope from the man from Hope.

It is a sad truth that inherent in visionary politics is the tendency toward psychological inflation or grandiosity—a shared grandiosity on the part of the leader and the people. In this case, the inflation turned out to be of mythic proportions and ended in disastrous political miscalculations. This was the reality. The potential creative tension between vision and reality could not hold and ended in collapse. I think it is reasonable to suggest as a psychological interpretation that not only did Clinton himself become inflated but also the Clintons as a couple became inflated—that is, the couple got caught in the power of an emerging new myth of equal and shared power between men and women. Together, they suffered the familiar archetypal pattern of such inflations—namely, soaring, visionary dreams ending in total collapse. The emotional and political price that the president, his wife, and his administration paid was severe. Many who had harnessed their dreams to the vision of universal health care were profoundly disappointed and disillusioned. They held the Clintons personally responsible for the failure of the health care reform initiative. Whatever the causes of the collapse might have been, it all came crashing to the ground as many such idealizations of leaders buoyed and fueled by the electorate's dreams are destined to do. The emotional hangover of such mythic visions linked to political failure is anger, cynicism, boredom, and disaffection. The only real measurable change that came from the promise of health care reform was a significant but transitory drop in the stock prices of drug companies that bore the brunt of Clinton's initial assault on the dragon of the health care establishment.

Several plausible interpretations can be made about the failure of the health care initiative, the role of the Clintons in that failure, and which archetypal mythic forces played themselves out in the political struggle. More than one mythic tale can be operating simultaneously in complex political battles. For instance, the epic Grail quest tells of a kingdom that is suffering, a Fisher King with a wound that won't heal, and a knight who goes in search of the Grail to bring a cure to both. This myth of the wounded would-be healer suits the Clinton mythopolitical picture as much as the hero's task of slaying the dragon. It does not take a big stretch of the imagination to think of Clinton as Parsifal going in search of the Grail to bring healing to the kingdom (the crisis in national health care) and his own wounded father king (the presidency). In our modern incarnation of the myth, the quest seems to have failed, and both the kingdom and the king are still very much in need of healing. Such is the complex intermingling of myth, psyche, and politics in the world—with more than a little economics thrown in.

Circumambulatio

Like politicians, analytical psychologists walk around the same material over and over again. Analytical psychologists call it *"circumambulatio."* Politicians call it the "campaign platform." Returning to the same issue over and over again is part of the slow digestion process of real integration— whether it be an individual integrating the symbolic material of a big dream over a lifetime or a nation integrating a racially divided population over many generations.

In that spirit, let's circle back to the starting point of this chapter—my dream of the skull from the early Christian era. The dream begins as a meditation on our own current global transformation with the advent of the millennium. In a sense, taken as a whole, the chapters in this book can be viewed as an extended group meditation on the dream image of the black monastic nun's skull—reflections on the dark, mysterious realm of the collective psyche, its past violent upheavals, current traumas, and future course. Gazing backward, we see that the early Christian era was a time of enormous turmoil—political, social, economic, spiritual. Even men and women's view of the cosmos was in flux. We too live in such an age, and the relationship between our deepest beliefs about ourselves and how we should structure our political life (even how to pay for our political life) raises many more questions than there are answers. How do we conceive of ourselves as a local, national, or global community when we have just learned that our sun is only one of fifty billion such stars in the Milky Way, and that the Milky Way itself is only one of more than fifty billion galaxies in the known universe? While our material resources are rapidly dwindling, our economy appears to be strong. The stock market—especially high-flying technology stocks—defy all traditional standards of valuation, and there is a healthy fear that what is so high may come crashing down. "Up and down, big and small" are playing tricks with our sense of value about money, our countries' roles in the world, and our shared sense of time and space. Almost daily we discover more about how small we are in the vastness of space and how interdependent we are on other nation states—truly a large dose of shifting perspectives for a young nation on a tiny planet.

With the rate of change itself rapidly accelerating and many of life's decisions and problems becoming ever more complex, many desperately search for clearer and simpler answers, which are often served up on the twin silver platters of political promises and religious panacea. Single-issue fundamentalism—whether it be clothed in religious or political dogma or both—becomes the order of the day on the right and the left, leaving a beleaguered and bland middle to wade through the muck in uncertainty. Over-simplification seems to be a human being's best and last defense against overwhelming complexity. C. G. Jung said many decades ago that modern man is in search of a myth(s) to live by. Perhaps today it might be more correct to say that post-modern man and woman is in search of a deconstructed myth(s) to live by. Such a search for integrative meaning frequently takes a political form or at least dresses itself up as if it were a political problem—a sort of metaphysical cross-dressing. Actually, the metaphor of cross-dressing is quite apt for a discussion of myth and politics because there is considerable identity confusion when we try to decide what is myth and what is politics and which is dressing up as which. The right to life/pro-abortion debate is a perfect example of how powerful and destructive this religious/political single-issue fundamentalism can become. All of life's complexities get condensed into and filtered through this profoundly disturbing debate, and in that crucible, we are asked to choose as if there is only one clear simple answer.

Myth and ritual

Let's return to the word *myth*. Myth's bad name comes from the titillating tales that are used to adorn or denigrate politicians' campaigns, celebrities' lives, nation states' ambitions, or the next-door neighbors' behavior. *Myth*, used in its colloquial meaning, usually signifies a misleading fiction or even a willfully distorted falsehood. Our use of it here might lead the reader to conclude: "I know the theme of this book. Politicians can't be trusted. They win votes by weaving myths about themselves and what they are going to do for us if they are elected. They poison the airwaves with tales of the sordid and evil wrongdoing of their opponents. It is all just myths. This book is going to explore the myths that are today's politics." (A previous book with just this aim was called *Reagan: The Man, The Myth*.)

Here, however, we are after a different level of mythopoetic perception from that of the false and superficial tales that shower every aspect of contemporary life—politics, sports, entertainment, business. Myth at this deeper level can be understood as the central unifying story that a group of people tells about itself—about its origins, its place in time and space, its trials and sufferings, and its means of sustaining, renewing, and re-creating itself through its vision of its role in the cycles of history, nature, and spirit. Myth at this level provides the foundation of ceremonial life, social life, and political life.

Politics, for example, is truly gripping when the myth of the times and its political processes are in creative relationship to one another. The Kennedy brothers—Jack with his grace and vision, Bobby with his gutsy existentialism—tapped into the potent mythological undercurrents of the 1960s and helped channel this energy into political activism for a brief creative burst that ended in the destruction of many lives and dreams. The opposite of this kind of potent alchemy between myth and politics is equally true. Nothing is more enervating to individuals than when the political processes of the body politic and the underlying stirrings of the collective psyche are not authentically related to one another.

Consider for a moment what I have come to call "the politics of empathy." With the growth of psychology as a popular frame of reference, our leaders have been learning that people want them to have feelings and, as a result, more and more politicians have been willing to reveal a feminine or feeling side of their personalities. There is something disturbing about this, because the capacity to manipulate deep emotions and images—what can be called archetypes—has always been the stock in trade of politicians and mass entertainers, who share a certain demagoguery. (Steven Spielberg and Bill Clinton are the perfect couple in this regard.) On the one hand, it is heartening that the collective psyche is moving toward a more genuine expression of compassion and empathy. The problem is that the present political enactment of this feminine archetypal potential ("I feel your pain") doesn't ring true. The words are right, but the tears are a crocodile's. Put another way, the persona of empathy is becoming part of the job of political and business leadership. This has given birth to a national industry of politicians and newscasters who serve as "disaster compassion consultants!" Their major function seems to be wearing the mask of compassion at an instant's notice when a plane crashes, a storm hits, or the country witnesses another murderous rampage in horror and fascination. In turn, our leaders as "compassion consultants" receive either higher ratings or more votes or both as a reward for their public display of empathy. As political leaders consciously seek "to connect" with the populace through "the politics of empathy," we become more and more aware of the real "disconnect" between our political processes and deeper mythological yearnings to link humans, nature, and spirit. Political pronouncements become empty sound bites, and fewer and fewer people feel gripped by an authentic intersection of myth and politics. Some politicians have even learned to use the words *vision* and *transformation* as if the repetitious magical incantation of the words themselves will create the belief in the electorate that they actually have a vision of the future or that they can bring about a much needed "transformation." But the underlying stirrings of the collective psyche and current political processes are rarely linked in an authentic connection that is believable to the general population.

The same can be said of ceremonial life, which is based on mythic foundations. It can be argued that the central collective ritual events of late twentieth-century America have become the Super Bowl, the Academy Awards, and the World Series, which are often more hype than substance, more letdown than exhilarating, more hollow than transforming. At a less grandiose level of modern ceremonial life, there has been a revolution in the conduct of marriages, funerals, and almost every other significant threshold ceremony in the past few decades that reflects the desire to link significant life passages in a real and personal way to age-old spiritual traditions. Many people no longer tolerate ceremonies that fail to honor and bring together both the personal and archetypal dimensions of life. They insist on a real connection between myth, psyche, and the important passages of their own lives. When politics fails to make that same connection, people abandon politics.

Women and men are born storytellers. When their stories are told and enacted in ritual often enough (the Roman numerals of the Super Bowl aspire through their repetition to attain this status), they become legends. And, if these legends in time become the spoken and unspoken backbone of a community's understanding of itself, we are truly in the realm of myth. A group's story of itself—its relation to nature and to the sacred, how its people are to relate to one another, and sometimes more importantly, how its people are to relate to those who are not part of its beginnings—gets told over and over again and becomes the central thread that binds generations together and gives them meaning and purpose. Whether it be the Jewish or Christian myth, America's twin myths of rugged individualism and the "melting pot," which have fused into the elusive American-dream marriage of capitalism and democracy, or the apparently dying Marxist-Leninist myth of Communism, these stories become the driving collective forces in the minds and hearts of people.

Women and men are also born political animals. As long as they have been telling their stories, they have also been enacting or fighting for their deepest beliefs and yearnings in political action. The contemporary language and discourse of politics seems barren and empty—perhaps occasionally riveting in the same way that we attend to or studiously avoid an O. J. Simpson saga, or witness in awe the enormous roller coaster of energy that propels a Newt Gingrich's rise and fall from popular grace. Whether it be the "New Covenant" or the "Contract with America," the promises of political platforms are undeliverable, while the pressures fueling the promises are enormous and uncontainable. Our cranked-up society with its incessant emphasis on peak performance creates ever-increasing expectations for athletic achievement, entrepreneurial creativity, stock market valuations, global high-technology networking, and even ever higher and higher spiritual attainment. Politicians as performers become empty vessels for filtering these insatiable appetites.

Shards

This project began with a question and a big dream a decade ago and, as I was searching for the right note to sound at the end of the introduction, another moving image emerged from the psyche. The new dream further oriented me to the problem of looking for the underlying myth(s) that might help draw a clearer picture of the contemporary relationship between myth and politics:

> *Wearing the robes of Asian Buddhist monks, I am part of an organized tour of Nepal or Tibet. Bill Bradley is a member of the group and is studying the sites with great interest and focus. We enter a vast underground space and soon I get separated from the group and wander around alone, lost and in fear. There is a sense of endless spaces of all sizes and shapes. One of them is a vast sacred place with a vaulted ceiling in the center—built centuries ago. Finally, I stumble out into the daylight, totally alone and profoundly disoriented. I see an information booth staffed by little old lady docents. They see how confused I am as I begin to empty my pockets of many glass shards that I have collected as I wandered from one space to another. The docents seem to know where they are and want to help orient me. As I look up behind the booth, I see signs pointing to Mount Everest and other places, and I begin to get a sense of where I am.*

Immediately on awakening, I remembered seeing a strikingly beautiful and powerful piece of sculpture by the modern German artist Anselm Kiefer. Entitled *Breaking of the Vessels*, it is Kiefer's attempt to make sense of the Holocaust as symbolized by *Kristallnacht*, the infamous night in November

1938 that the Nazis smashed the glass out of the windows of Jewish-owned stores. Kiefer's art wrestles with the awful intersection of myth and politics in the Nazi era by linking *Kristallnacht* to the creation myth of the Jewish mystical tradition of the *Lurianic Kabbalah*. He has constructed a large sculpture of steel, copper, and hundreds of shattered shards of glass that spill out onto the gallery floor. The sculpture evokes the Kabbalistic vision of the "breaking of the vessels," in which the original oneness of creation is shattered into broken fragments. Kiefer physically frames the political atrocity of *Kristallnacht* in the context of this primal breaking of the vessels. The fragments simultaneously carry the divine sparks of the once-whole world soul and symbolize the introduction of evil into creation. The shards are only fragments of what was originally whole.

Senator Bradley's question years ago began my search for a unifying collective myth(s) that might give meaning to contemporary political life. But the dream suggests that in undertaking a tour into the collective unconscious, I get confused, lost, and frightened as I travel through vast and tiny underground places. What I find in my pockets as I emerge above ground is little bits and pieces of the divine spark from many traditions, but none of them is whole—although as broken fragments they suggest that there was a time when they were part of a whole. What is orienting, paradoxically, is the knowledge that: (1) There isn't a contemporary unifying collective myth; (2) there are fragments of what was once whole to be discovered in many places; (3) it is useless to look for a unifying myth in one place or tradition—like politics alone; (4) but, one shouldn't give up on the fragments, which allude at least to the possibility of an underlying spiritual image of wholeness, bits and pieces of which may be found in many places. And does Mount Everest still stand for that daunting, but perhaps attainable wholeness of Self, in spite of the pollution that now tracks right up to its summit?

Notes

1 Introduction to *The Vision Thing: Myth, Politics, and Psyche in the World*, ed. Thomas Singer, 1–18 (London and New York: Routledge, 2000). Reprinted with permission of the publisher.

2 *Oxford Dictionary of Quotations:* Keats quote #21 from letter to his brothers, G. and T. Keats, letter 32, 21 December 1817, reading: "Negative capability, that is, when a man is capable of being in uncertainties, mysteries, doubts, without any irritable reaching after facts and reason."

3 C. G. Jung, "The Relations Between the Ego and the Unconscious" (1928), *The Collected Works of C. G. Jung,* vol. 7, *Two Essays on Analytical Psychology* (Princeton: Princeton University Press, 1969), ¶235.

2 The cultural complex and archetypal defenses of the collective spirit

Baby Zeus, Elian Gonzales, Constantine's sword, and other holy wars

From *The San Francisco Jung Institute Library Journal* 20, no. 4, 2002.[1]

In 2000, I was invited to co-present with Donald Kalsched at a conference in Bozeman, Montana. Dr. Kalsched's work focused on the inner world of trauma with the elaboration of his ground-breaking Jungian model of the forces unleashed in the psyches of severely traumatized individuals. At the same time, I was becoming more attuned to the powerful forces unleashed in the psyches of groups under conditions of severe stress. At the Bozeman conference, Kalsched and I discovered a mutual interest in the Daimones when I showed a slide of these protective guardians surrounding Baby Zeus. I applied Kalsched's notion of the archetypal defenses of the personal spirit to the notion of archetypal defenses of the group spirit and later elaborated it in this chapter.

Much as an airline pilot gives the passengers a brief synopsis of the flight plan, I would like to provide an itinerary for this intuitive flight so that some of the landmarks along the way have a context. The series of seemingly unrelated historical episodes that I will be highlighting are linked together by a kind of intuitive logic that seeks to sketch an extension of traditional Jungian theory. Indeed, this chapter is meant to be a "sketch" in the same way that an artist or architect would render a preliminary drawing of a work in progress that will be elaborated over time.

Jung's earliest work at the Burghölzli led to the development of his theory of complexes, which even now forms the foundation of the day-to-day clinical work of analytical psychology. In fact, there was a time when the founders of the Jungian tradition considered calling it "complex psychology." Later, Joseph Henderson created a much needed theoretical space between the personal and archetypal levels of the psyche, which he called the "cultural level of the psyche." This cultural level of the psyche exists in both the conscious and the unconscious. Elaborating Jung's theory of complexes as it manifests itself in the cultural level of the psyche—conscious and unconscious—is the goal of this chapter. In the effort to sketch this idea, we will be taking a tour that includes stops at Jane Harrison's study of early Greek religion, Elian Gonzales's gripping story of loss and political upheaval, James Carroll's study of anti-Semitism in the history of the Catholic Church, current manifestations of the primal psychoanalytic split between Jung and Freud, and finally a brief commentary on the al Qaeda attack on the West and the "God Bless America" response. All of these episodes help illustrate the reality of cultural complexes and elucidate a specific type of cultural complex in which archetypal defenses of the collective spirit play a primary role.

Jane Harrison's *Themis*

In 1912, when Jane Harrison published *Themis: A Study of the Social Origins of Greek Religion,* her stunning exploration of matriarchal pre-Olympian Greek religion, Jung's notion of archetypes and the collective unconscious had not yet been conceived.[2] One can almost feel those seminal insights struggling to get born as Harrison weaves threads of anthropology, classical studies, archaeology, sociology, and psychology. Her book reads like a detective story as she seeks to discover and piece together the origins of early Greek religion. Her work is named for, inspired by, and presided over by the goddess Themis who embodies the earliest Western ideas of civility and community. Mention of Harrison's book is a fitting place to begin this contemporary piece of psychological theory making, because it is not only in her spirit of the detective piecing together bits and pieces of "evidence" to get at a whole that this chapter is undertaken, but also in fact one of the central images from her work actually gave birth to this project.

Baby Zeus and Elian Gonzales

The contemporary context of this inquiry begins in exactly the same place as Jane Harrison's: with a fascination about the origins, underlying meaning, and power of collective emotion. Harrison was gripped by the force of collective emotion in its capacity to create gods, social order, and a meaningful link between humans, nature, and spirit in pre-Olympian Greece. I am equally fascinated by the power of collective emotion to create gods, devils, political movements, and social upheaval/transformation in our times. Harrison did not have the concept of the collective unconscious and its archetypes in which to ground her ideas about the origin of social and religious life in early Greece. But she was a keen observer of art, ritual, and especially the degree to which collective emotion and its enthusiasms seemed to generate a coherent mythos that linked the natural and social order into a coherent whole. At the epicenter of her quest was the glorious mystery of "The Hymn of the Kouretes." Through Harrison's eyes, the image of Baby Zeus surrounded by the protective young male warriors, the Kouretes, comes to life and the very foundations of early Greek religion are unveiled:

> Io, Kouros most Great, I give thee hail, Kronian, Lord of all that is wet and gleaming, thou art come at the head of thy Daimones. To Dike for the Year, Oh, march, and rejoice in the dance and song,
>
> That we make to thee with harps and pipes mingled together, and sing as we come to a stand at thy well-fenced altar.
>
> [Io, etc.]
>
> For here the shielded Nurturers took thee, a child immortal, from Rhea, and with noise of beating feet hid thee away.
>
> [Io, etc.]
>
> And the Horai began to be fruitful year by year and Dike to possess mankind, and all wild living things were held about by wealth-loving Peace.
>
> [Io, etc.]
>
> To us also leap for full jars, and leap for fleecy flocks, and leap for fields of fruit, and for hives to bring increase.
>
> [Io, etc.]
>
> Leap for our Cities, and leap for our sea-borne ships, and leap for our young citizens and for godly Themis.[3]

Baby Zeus, who is here referred to as "Kouros most Great," was secretly stolen away from his nursery and handed over to the Kouretes for protection by his mother Rhea, wife of Kronos. She did not want him to suffer the same fate as his older brothers and sisters—namely, to be eaten by his father, Kronos. The young god was shielded from destruction by the Kouretes who, in their youthful energy, leap for the gods and secure the safety and renewal of the crops, the animals, the cities, the ships, the "young citizens," and for godly Themis.

Several thousand years later, in our time, young Elian Gonzales was miraculously plucked from the very sea in which his mother had just drowned. She perished trying to bring him to the "promised land," and within a short period of time, he became the center of a psychic and political drama that stirred the emotions of at least two nations. The response of Elian's Cuban-American relatives and their community made little sense to most Americans, who do not share the same historical experience or mythic story of their origins, survival, and renewal.

Most well-intentioned non-Cuban-Americans seized by this tragic story felt that the motherless child should be reunited as quickly as possible with his loving father, even if he happened to live in Castro's Cuba. Most people found themselves thinking: "These Cuban-Americans are crazy. Isn't it obvious that Elian should be returned to his surviving parent?" Indeed, it was the extraordinary power of the nonrational collective emotion of the Cuban-Americans that caught my attention. "Why are they behaving so 'irrationally'?" I asked myself. It wasn't until I happened by chance to glance again at the image of Baby Zeus from Jane Harrison's 1912 book that I was able to find a missing link to the story that allowed me to make some sense (at least for myself) of what seemed so irrational and yet was being deeply felt not just by the Cuban-Americans, but all the other people caught up in this extraordinary drama. What if Baby Zeus and Elian Gonzales are part of the same story? What if they are linked by a mythic form or archetypal pattern out of which are generated a story line, primal images, and deeply powerful, nonrational collective emotion?

Elian Gonzales's miraculous second birth, or rebirth, as he was plucked from the waters puts him in the realm of the divine child (like Moses), like the young god who carries all the hopes for the future of a people that sees itself as having been traumatized by a life of cruel oppression. He, too, in his vulnerable state of youthful divinity, needs to be protected from destruction by his warrior cousins who rally to his defense. For Elian Gonzales's "shielded nurturers" to willingly return him to Castro's Cuba (because now, as a young god, he belongs to all his people, not just his personal family) would be equivalent to the Kouretes sending Baby Zeus back to Kronos. In the mythic imagination of the Cuban-American collective, Fidel Castro is the same as Kronos—a destructive father god who would eat his own son, the youthful god. Elian Gonzales's "crazy cousins" are not so crazy after all. They are the Kouretes, dancing in the frenzy of a collective emotion that seeks to form a protective circle or shield around their young god.

The force/libido providing the energy to fuel these incredible sagas comes from the collective emotion mobilized by the plight of a gravely endangered, vulnerable (divine) child who symbolizes the hopes of an entire people. The inevitable archetypal coupling of the endangered divine child and the protective warrior Kouretes who surround him are at the heart of the story I want to tell and the theory I want to advance.

Donald Kalsched and the archetypal defense of the personal spirit

Donald Kalsched's groundbreaking work in *The Inner World of Trauma: Archetypal Defenses of the Personal Spirit* forms the next major building block of this chapter.[4] In the summer of 2000, I participated in a conference with Dr. Kalsched in Montana. His paper focused on the inner world of trauma, while my presentation was more about the outer domain where myth, psyche, and politics intersect—a subject that I have explored with others in *The Vision Thing: Myth, Politics and Psyche in the World*.[5] I had just stumbled into an imaginal connection between Baby Zeus and Elian Gonzales and was using the image of Baby Zeus surrounded by the Kouretes to illustrate the reality of the collective psyche and the power of collective emotion to generate living myths. Kalsched had not seen this particular image before, and he startled with both surprise and instant recognition at the lively representation of the warriors defending Baby Zeus. He immediately knew who they were, correctly identifying them as the Daimones. Indeed, the Kouretes are also known as the Daimones: "Io, Kouros most Great … thou art come at the head of thy Daimones."[6]

These prototypes or original Daimones surrounding Baby Zeus are in the same lineage as those characters whom Kalsched a few millennia later would identify as the "archetypal defenses of the personal spirit." If one thinks of this image psychologically as a portrait of the endangered psyche, one sees clearly that the Daimones have the intrapsychic function of protecting a vulnerable, traumatized youthful Self—be it Baby Zeus, Elian Gonzales, or any other less famous wounded soul. As Kalsched has elaborated, the Daimones have the function of protecting the "personal spirit" when the individual is endangered. These same Daimones also have the function of protecting the "collective spirit" of the group when it is endangered—be it Cuban-Americans, Jews, African Americans, LGBTs, or any other traumatized "group soul." The Daimones are as active in the psychological "outer" world of group life and the protection of its "collective spirit" as they are in the inner individual world of trauma and the protection of "the personal spirit." Perhaps they even found their earliest expression in group life rather than that of a single person, when the psychology of the individual was less developed and the survival of the group more in the forefront.

We have come to appreciate the Daimones again through the Jungian route of recognizing their role in the inner world of trauma. Whether it be in the inner/outer world of the individual or the inner/outer world of the group, the Daimones can serve both a vital self-protective function and can raise havoc with the fury of their attacks directed inwardly in self-torture and outwardly in impenetrability, hostility, and ruthlessness. The fortuitous recognition of the connection between Baby Zeus and Elian Gonzales led me to consider an extension of Kalsched's insights into what might best be summarized in this reformulation of his book's title: "The Group World of Trauma: Archetypal Defenses of the Collective Spirit." Extending Kalsched's ideas into the realm of group experience and linking these ideas with the notion of a "cultural complex" is the goal of this chapter.

I will briefly summarize the central elements of Kalsched's formulations in order to lay a foundation for considering them in relation to group processes.

1. Trauma alone does not shatter the psyche. The psyche shatters itself through its own self-defense system. In a sense, the psyche's defense system is as traumatogenic as the original trauma because its focus is on survival and it interprets any attempt to grow and individuate as dangerous and needing to be punished. According to the Daimon-Protector defense system, reaching out beyond a closed system of certainty exposes the personal spirit to further traumatization.

2. This occurs because the "daimonic defense system" is unleashed against the psyche for the purpose of converting annihilation anxiety into a more manageable fear. This self-protective mechanism preserves a fearful ego in the face of shattering trauma rather than permitting the ego to be annihilated altogether. This self-protective mechanism, which results in self-attack, can be likened to the autoimmune system having gone haywire when it turns its substantial arsenal of defenses back on one's own tissues. Fragmentation of the psyche is the result.

3. The Daimon-Protector defenses are internalized representations of the original perpetrators of the trauma. Even more than that, they are archaic, typical, and archetypal.

4. Following the psyche's fragmenting, a false self takes up residence in the outer world. This false self can function well enough in ordinary situations, although it is most likely to break down in intimate relationships. It can also take on a caretaker function as well as become a compliant, good adult.

5. On the other side of the fragmentation, the true self goes into inner hibernation behind the ferociously protective barrier of the Daimones—which can be alternately protective and torturing.

6. The individual has very little access to effective aggression in the world.

7. The shadow of being a traumatized victim is the tendency toward an imperious sense of entitlement and its accompanying demands for

reparation. A false, imperial self can take root that demands love, respect, sexual pleasure, freedom, and happiness.

8. At the heart of this fragmented psychic "balance" resides a vulnerable, wounded child surrounded by an archaic defense system that can alternate between sheltering protection and ruthless torturing of the self and others.

What if this highly schematized outline of the psyche's response to trauma applies as much to a group's response to trauma as it does to the individual's? The same dynamics so elegantly described by Kalsched may come alive in the traumatized group psyche as well as in the private horror of a traumatized individual. The traumatized group may develop a cohort of protector/persecutor leaders who function like the Kouretes protecting Baby Zeus or the Cuban-American relatives protecting Elian Gonzales. The traumatized group spirit may well be subject to the same nurturing protection and/or violent torture at the hands of its Daimones leaders. All of the group's defenses are mobilized in the name of a self-care system that is designed to protect the injured divine child of the group identity as well as to protect the group "ego" from a terrifying sense of imminent annihilation.

The group may develop a defensive system akin to the individual, but in this case its goal is to protect the group or collective spirit rather than the individual spirit. Such a traumatized group presents only a "false self" to the world, and the world cannot "see" the group in its more authentic and vulnerable identity. The rest of the world, which is not part of the traumatized group, may see only the more hardened "daimonic" front men or women and respond to their aggression and impenetrability as if they were the whole group. Such a traumatized group with its defenses of the collective spirit may find itself living with a history that spans several generations, several centuries, or even millennia with repetitive wounding experiences that fix these patterns of behavior and emotion into what analytical psychologists have come to know as "complexes." The group complexes create bipolar fields in the same way that personal complexes activate or constellate in external reality the very splits that have splintered the inner world. The traumatized life of the group gets incorporated into the inner life of the individual through a group complex—which may be mistaken for or get confused with a personal complex. How do we learn to distinguish the cultural or group level of the complex from the more "personal" level of the complex with its archetypal core? Before we address the implications of these assertions and the questions that follow from them, there is a missing building block in the argument that I am assembling.

Joseph Henderson: The cultural level of the psyche and the reality of group complexes

One of Joseph Henderson's many seminal contributions to analytical psychology has been to delineate more carefully the space in the psyche between the personal and archetypal levels of psychological experience. He has called this the "cultural level" of the psyche and has elaborated a typology for that level of reality: social, aesthetic, philosophic, and spiritual.[7] For Jungians, Henderson's work has opened the theoretical door to the vast realm of human experience that inhabits the psychical space between our most personal and our most archetypal levels of being in the world. For example, there is surely something in cultural life that nourishes us like a mother but is neither our personal mother nor archetypal Demeter. Henderson's elaboration of the cultural level of the psyche has made greater space for the outer world of group life to have a home in the inner Jungian world and allowed the inner Jungian world to recognize more fully the outer world of social and cultural experience.

Extending Henderson's notion of the "cultural level" of the psyche, Sam Kimbles has begun to speak of "cultural complexes" or "group complexes" in his essay, "The Cultural Complex and The Myth of Invisibility" in *The Vision Thing*.[8] These complexes function in that intermediate realm between the personal and archetypal level of the psyche, partaking of both but also being absolutely unique in that their content and activity is the bridge and link between the individual, society, and the archetypal realms. Cultural complexes are at the heart of the conflicts between many groups and are expressed in group life all the time: politically, economically, sociologically, geographically, and religiously. For example, one simply has to think of the struggles between Christians and Jews, blacks and whites, gays and straights, men and women, to begin to imagine how potent are the individual and collective processes activated by "cultural complexes." When these complexes are triggered, all of the emotion of the personal and archetypal realm gets channeled through group life and its experience. Cultural complexes are lived out in group life, and they are internalized in the psyche of individuals.

Just as Henderson opened up the vast intermediate realm between the personal and archetypal, Sam Kimbles and I hope that our work on cultural complexes can help us begin to recognize the difference between individual and cultural complexes. For many analytical psychologists, Jung's theory of complexes and its subsequent elaboration forms the cornerstone of the day-to-day work of psychotherapy and analysis. Like the Freudian theory of defenses, Jung's notion of complexes provides a handle for understanding the nature of intrapsychic and interpersonal conflict.

Complexes express themselves in powerful moods and repetitive behaviors. They resist our most heroic efforts at consciousness, and they tend to collect experience that confirms their preexisting view of the world. Complexes are the psychological analog of the vegetative biological systems, such as those that carry out digestion or maintain blood pressure. An activated personal complex can have its own body language and tone of voice. It can operate beneath the level of consciousness; we do not have to think about complexes for them to carry out their autonomous processes of structuring and filtering our experience of ourselves and others. A further characteristic of complexes, elegantly elaborated by John Perry, is that they tend to be bipolar or consist of two parts.[9] Most often, when a complex is activated, one part of the bipolar complex attaches itself to the ego and the other part gets projected onto a suitable other. For instance, in a typical negative father complex, a rebellious son inevitably finds the authoritarian father in every teacher, coach, or boss who provides a suitable hook for the negative projection. This bipolarity of the complex leads to an endless round of repetitive skirmishes with the illusory other—who may or may not fit the bill perfectly. Finally, complexes can be recognized by the simplistic certainty of a world view and one's place in it that they offer us, in the face of the otherwise very difficult task of holding the tension of conflicting and not easily reconcilable opposites. A colleague likes to tell a story about herself that well illustrates this psychological fact. After a day of "holding the opposites" in the office with her analysands, she enjoys watching John Wayne movies in which it is clear who the bad guys and the good guys are. She points out that it is far easier to settle for the certainty of a complex than wrestle with the emotional ambiguity of inner and outer reality that is constantly challenging the ego.

Cultural complexes structure emotional experience and operate in the personal and collective psyche in much the same way as individual complexes, although their content might be quite different. Like individual complexes, cultural complexes tend to be repetitive, autonomous, resist consciousness, and collect experience that confirms their historical point of view. Cultural complexes also tend to be bipolar, so that when they are activated the group ego becomes identified with one part of the unconscious complex, while the other part is projected out onto the suitable hook of another group. Individuals and groups in the grip of a particular cultural complex automatically take on a shared body language and postures or express their distress in similar somatic complaints. Finally, like personal complexes, cultural complexes provide a simplistic certainty about the group's place in the world in the face of otherwise conflicting and ambiguous uncertainties.

Because of its primary focus on the individuation process, the Jungian tradition has tended to emphasize the development of the individual out of his or her particular collective experience, but has not been particularly clear or helpful in differentiating individual from cultural complexes. Certainly Jung and his followers have had a sense of different cultural types, which is evident, for example, in Jung's discussion of national personality characteristics in *Memories, Dreams, Reflections*.[10] But this perception of different cultural types has never adequately been linked to Jung's theory of complexes or to how these differences get incorporated into the psyche of the individual and the group. Both in the clinical work of individual analysis and in the broader Jungian tradition of archetypal and cultural commentary, it is of enormous potential benefit to begin to make clearer distinctions between an individual complex and a cultural complex. It offers both the individual and groups the opportunity of not having to telescope or condense everything into the personal or archetypal realm—but to recognize the legitimate cultural and group contributions to their struggles, suffering, and meaning.

One can easily imagine how the individual's ego can identify with a cultural complex as a defense against a more painful and isolating personal complex. It is far easier to split off one's individual suffering (or to see it all as a result of group trauma) and get caught up in a mass movement than it is to carry the burden of one's individual pain. Within analytical psychology itself, there is a growing tradition of archetypal commentary on cultural experience that tends to neglect how the individual relates to the culture through more personal experiences and complexes. Archetypal commentary on the culture's underlying myths and failings can easily camouflage the need to work hard at grappling with individual complexes. Differentiating the personal, cultural, and archetypal level of complexes requires careful attention to each of these realms, without condensing or telescoping one into the other, as if one were more real or true than the other. Finally, cultural complexes are based on repetitive, historical group experiences that have taken root in the collective psyche of groups and in the individual/collective psyches of individual members of the group. One can think of cultural complexes as the fundamental building blocks and content of an inner sociology.

Cultural complexes and archetypal defenses of the collective spirit: Constantine's sword

Donald Kalsched's work offers a compelling model of how the individual psyche responds to trauma in its defense of the self. Can his model be extended to include specific categories of group behavior and allow us to see a bit more clearly the structure and content of certain types of group or cultural complexes? Of course, I am not suggesting that all cultural complexes behave in the particular model of a traumatized, vulnerable child and pro-tective/torturer Daimones, as described by Kalsched. But many of them do. There are two separate but related points that I want to emphasize here:

1. There is a continuum in the content and structure of complexes that ranges from the personal to the cultural to the archetypal. At the same time, some complexes have become such a part of a group's identity over time and repetitive experience that the cultural level of the complex becomes dominant or paramount, even in the psyche of an individual. Individuals are frequently swallowed whole by the group complex that has come to define their ethnic, religious, racial, gender, or other pri-mary sense of identity.

2. Sometimes groups as a whole behave as if they are in the grip of a spe-cific type of cultural complex. This type of cultural complex mobilizes in the group's behavior, emotion, and life a defensive self-care system akin to that described in individuals by Kalsched. In the group version of the complex, however, the goal of the self-care defensive system is the protection of the collective spirit, not the personal spirit. The Daimones are mobilized to protect the traumatized divine child or other symbolic carrier of the collective spirit of the group and can do so with a mixture of sheltering kindness and persecutory attack, which directed inwardly results in self-loathing and directed outwardly results in impenetrability and hostilities to other groups.

One has only to glance at the daily newspaper to see the proliferation in popular culture of these group complexes at work. Indeed, it has almost become a national sport for traumatized groups to send out Daimones (attorneys and others) to attack the general public for neglecting the entitled interests of their particular victimized group. A large part of the public has grown weary of this institutionalization of group defenses of the collective spirit. Frequently members of the victimized group are so identified with themselves as wounded divine children that it is hard for them to under-stand how their Daimones/Protectors, embodied in public spokespersons/ attackers, are perceived as an aggressive, destructive, hostile turnoff by those who are not identified with their plight. In the psychic arena of our global group life, it is as if every group is "loaded for bear"—out there with their group trauma, their group divine child, and their group Daimones (protectors/persecutors) ready to swing into action.

I have already offered one such contemporary example of a cultural com-plex that was activated in the defense of the collective spirit—that of the Cuban-Americans and Elian Gonzales. But to further amplify this cluster of ideas, I want to focus on another stunning example of the dynamic interplay between cultural complex and archetypal defenses of the collective spirit. In this example one gets a rare glimpse at the continuum of complex from individual to cultural to archetypal, and one can also see how the defenses of the collective spirit became a monster. It would be easiest to focus on groups such as LGBTs, African Americans, women, the disabled, and other obviously disenfranchised and historically traumatized peoples, to see how the dynamics of the cultural complex and defenses of the collective spirit play out. But a recent book by James Carroll entitled *Constantine's Sword: The Church and the Jews, A History* suggested to me that the same dynamics can be seen in the Catholics, a group that few would now characterize as a disenfranchised and traumatized minority.[11]

Constantine's Sword is a history of Christian—more specifically Catholic—anti-Semitism. Starting with the old Christian belief that Jews were the "Christ-killers," Carroll systematically examines layer upon layer of historical event, political context, emotional climate, theological justification, and psychological consequence. He begins his narrative by describing Catholic and Jewish reactions to a memorial cross placed at Auschwitz as the latest episode in a stormy and violent two-millennia relationship. His reflections on the Auschwitz cross are placed in the context of his memories of growing up in Germany right after World War II and his own early childhood belief that Jews were, in fact, "Christ-killers." After carefully probing the details of his Catholic upbringing, Carroll opens an in-depth exploration of the entire historical sweep of Catholic-Jewish relations. Carroll does not claim to tell the whole story of the development of Catholicism or Judaism or of the relations between the two religions.

Let us briefly follow the thread of Carroll's work. On the personal side, the early development of his faith took place in the epicenter of the most traumatic event of modern Western history—the Holocaust. Carroll's father was commander of the United States Air Force in Germany immediately following World War II. The family lived at headquarters in Wiesbaden, Germany. Accompanying his devoutly Catholic mother, an adolescent Jim Carroll traveled to many of the important Catholic shrines of Western Europe. Through his deep love of his mother and his intimate knowledge of her suffering because of the crippling illness (polio) of his brother, Carroll developed a faith rooted in the cross, the mother, and the suffering son. Growing up in post-Nazi Germany, Carroll saw much of the great Catholic tradition and the devastation of World War II, but learned little of the Holocaust and the suffering of the Jews at that time. To the Catholic boy, Jews were still identified simply as "Christ-killers."

This is where Carroll's personal complex and the cultural complex get all mixed up—not just in his history but in the two-thousand-year history that he sets out to explore in this book. The Christian religion that nurtured a youth aspiring to the priesthood placed suffering and traumatic death at the center of the Western collective experience, indeed at the center of all human history. And right at the very heart of that story, as he heard it, was the belief that the Jews were responsible for the suffering and traumatic death of the young god. This belief—reinforced through a long history of theological amplification and political, social, and religious persecution—has fueled a virulent collective emotion of loathing and rage that has burned without interruption for centuries. Collective emotion fuels the Daimones' dance around Baby Zeus; collective emotion fuels the Cuban-Americans' dance around Elian Gonzales; and two millennia of collective emotion demanding vengeance on the "Christ-killers" fuels a long line of Daimones from the Crusaders to the Nazis.

One of the many surprising revelations of Carroll's historical journey is that the suffering and traumatic death of the young god for which the Jews have been held responsible has not always been at the center of Christian faith. Indeed, the cult of the cross does not seem to come to center stage until the time of Constantine in the early part of the fourth century CE. Even today, the Eastern Orthodox Church places more emphasis on the mystery of the resurrection or rebirth than on the traumatic death symbolized by the crucifixion. Imagine for a moment what the history of the Western world might have been like if suffering and trauma had not been at the center of the story that the West has told about itself since the time of Christ. Of course, the fact is that the traumatic death of the crucifixion has been at the center of Western orthodoxy since the time of Constantine.

When Constantine was crossing the Milvian Bridge to attack Rome in 312 CE, he had a vision and a conversion experience in which his sword and the cross became one. Carroll writes:

> The place of the cross in the Christian imagination changed with Constantine. "He said that about noon, when the day was already beginning to decline"—this is Eusebius's account of Constantine's own report of what he saw in the sky on the eve of the battle above the Milvian Bridge—"he saw with his own eyes the trophy of a cross of light in the heavens, above the sun, and bearing the inscription CONQUER BY THIS." The story goes on to say that Constantine then assembled his army—"He sat in the midst of them, and described to them the figure of the sign he had seen"—and gave them the new standard to carry into battle. "Now it was made in the following manner. A long spear, over-laid with gold, formed the figure of the cross by means of a transverse bar laid over it." As we saw, the army behind this standard did conquer, and Constantine, so Eusebius heard him say, was thus convinced of the truth of Christianity. "The emperor constantly made use of this sign of

salvation as a safeguard against every adverse and hostile power, and commanded that others similar to it should be carried at the head of all his armies."[12]

Constantine became a Christian and the Christian faith found a protector/persecutor/Daimon of the first order. At that moment, the symbol of traumatic injury—the cross—and its avenging protector in the form of Constantine's sword got married. I would argue that this symbolic marriage of cross and sword is an example of the historical emergence of an "archetypal defense of the collective spirit." It might be helpful at this point to remind the reader of what I said about Baby Zeus in the early part of this chapter: the inevitable archetypal coupling of the endangered divine child and the protective warrior Daimones who surround him are at the heart of the story I want to tell and the theory I want to advance. Christ is not Baby Zeus and he is not a child; but in the mythoreligious imagination of the West, he is in that lineage of divine beings who has found potent Daimones/Protectors who commit unimaginable atrocities in his name.

Groups go on the attack in defense of their collective spirit when they fear being annihilated, especially if there is a history of trauma at their beginnings. The Christian story begins in trauma. Some three hundred years after the crucifixion of Christ, the suffering divine being finds his archetypal and historical Daimon/Protector/Persecutor in Constantine, from whose sword Carroll traces a direct line to the Crusades, the Inquisition, and finally the Holocaust. One can argue, in summary, that at the heart of the central cultural complex and narrative event of the Western Christian psyche is the emergence of an archetypal defense of the collective spirit, the central features of which include

1. Traumatic injury to a vulnerable divine being representing the group spirit
2. Fear of annihilation of the group spirit
3. Emergence of avenging protector/persecutor defense of the collective spirit

In the Christian coupling of cross and sword, the archetypal defense of the collective spirit turned all of its more shadowy aggressive energy outward, and one sees self-righteousness rather than self-hatred. (Note that obviously this is not the whole story of Christianity nor of Judaism since Constantine. Rather, it is following one thread only that has contributed to a particularly potent/virulent cultural complex.) The Jews bore the brunt of this two-thousand-year-old archetypal defense of the collective spirit and to some degree mirrored its aggressiveness in self-hatred, until Zionism and the

Holocaust gave birth to a generation of Jews that could say with equally aggressive self-affirmation: "Never Again." "Never Again" grew out of unimaginable human suffering and the resolve to protect the Jewish collective spirit at any cost, giving birth to a whole new generation of Jewish Daimones whom the Palestinians and Israelis know quite well.

Carroll's book, from one perspective then, can be viewed as the extraordinary effort of an individual to unravel his personal complexes from a cultural complex that, until consciously examined, are in fact so interwoven and continuous that it would be impossible to know where the personal part of the complex ends and the cultural part begins. Carroll would not describe his effort in the language of Jung's complex theory and analytical psychology, but it is clear that all of his considerable emotional and intellectual passions have been devoted to teasing out the different levels of personal, cultural, and archetypal conflict that are at the heart of his history of the Catholics and the Jews. Carroll's personal journey to free himself from the myth of the Jews as "Christ-killers" and all of the collective emotion that has been ignited in the name of that belief, is deeply entangled with the two-thousand-year history of animosity, misunderstanding, persecution, and trauma that characterize Jewish-Christian relations. One of the most important aspects of his book from a Jungian perspective is that he gives us an X-ray of the layering of the personal, cultural, and archetypal dimensions of the complex he is probing. This approach opens him up to criticism from more "objective" historians, some of whom have dismissed his work as too "personal."

Indeed, Carroll's search for historical objectivity begins with an examination of his own subjectivity. In my opinion, the objectivity he gains from the hard introspective work of looking at his own personal and family history is more authentic than the carefully cultivated dispassionate objectivity of a conventional historian who is trained to refrain from injecting his own experience and biases into the story. Carroll's method is truer to our own experience of how the personal and cultural get all mixed up in the unconscious of our family lives and in the cultural and religious history of humankind. Paradoxically, by publicly wrestling with the personal dimensions of his development as a devout Catholic, he leads us to a profound consideration of the unfolding of the historical relations between Catholics and Jews. This is because Carroll's personal revelations naturally evoke and invite us to consider our own personal and cultural complexes in relation to this history. And through the window of his story opening our story, we are initiated or re-initiated into a horrifying story of the last two thousand years. From one point of view, then, this book is a history of a personal complex set in the context of a two-millennia cultural complex, as well as a two-millennia cultural complex set in the context of a personal complex.

Never again and the history of Jung and Freud: A cultural complex even closer to home

Of course, the traumatized (that is, crucified) Christ as the carrier of the collective spirit in need of archetypal defenses in the form of the sword, the Crusades, the Inquisition, the pogroms, and ultimately the Holocaust are just one side of the history of this horrific cultural complex. Like other personal and cultural complexes, it is part of a bipolar pair, and the other side—the Jewish—has its own story of trauma, fear of annihilation, and the emergence of avenging protector/persecutor Daimones who defend the collective spirit.

One has to look no further than our own tradition of psychoanalysis— Jungian and Freudian alike—and how it gets told from one generation to the next to see the power of such cultural complexes (stories) in which the archetypal defenses of the collective spirit have been mobilized—this time in the defense of the Jewish collective spirit rather than the Christian collective spirit. An example of this potent phenomenon flared at a recent conference on the history of psychoanalysis. Seen from the perspective of the Christian/Jewish complex detailed in Carroll's book, the Jung-Freud conflict and its historical unfolding is just a short chapter in the ongoing saga of how not just individuals but the whole history of groups gets swallowed by even larger cultural complexes and their archetypal defenses of the collective spirit.

Thomas Kirsch, a past president of the International Association for Analytical Psychology and a Jew, is particularly sensitive to the Christian/ Jewish component of the conflict between Jung and Freud. Kirsch literally grew up with it as part of his childhood. He knew well that Jung had been anointed "the Christian Crown-Prince" of psychoanalysis by the Jewish psychoanalytic father Freud. He knew well that Freud had hoped Jung would take the psychoanalytic word from his small Jewish circle in Vienna to the non-Jewish, Christian world of Zürich and beyond to the West. Kirsch also knew that Jung's bitter split from Freud, seen through the lens of the Christian/Jewish cultural complex, could be viewed as one more betrayal and "murder" of a Jew by a Christian. Kirsch's own father, James Kirsch, had to spend much of his professional career explaining in a careful, scholarly way that Jung was not a Nazi.

Part of what must have motivated the elder Kirsch's lifelong, passionate defense of Jung had to be his desire to make it absolutely clear that he himself had not betrayed the Jews by following Jung. This must have been acutely painful for the elder Kirsch, because not only was he a Jungian and Jewish, but also he was a German Jew. How can you be German, Jewish, and Jungian?

Once you fall into the grip of a cultural complex, guilt by association rules in the collective psyche. The Kirsches knew this as German, Jewish Jungians. Jim Carroll knew this as an Irish Catholic who began to discover in his adolescence what had been done to the Jews in the name of Christ and the cross. The "logic" of a cultural complex has the same nonrational collective emotional power that led the Cuban-Americans to a fierce defense of Elian Gonzales. The goal of this emotion and "logic" is to protect the collective spirit. In the case of Jung, the "logic" of the Jewish argument against him and the emotional drive to dismiss his followers is primal and, stated bluntly, runs something like the following: "Jung was a Nazi. If you follow Jung, you are anti-Semitic at best and participated at least indirectly in the Holocaust. Jungians favor the annihilation of our people. We must vigorously defend ourselves against them, and as they would annihilate us, we must deny their existence." Put in the broader perspective of the Christian/Jewish conflict explored in Carroll's book, it has been common for traumatized Jews to dismiss Jung and his followers as part of the long line of those who followed Constantine's sword and initiated the Crusades, the Inquisition, the pogroms, and the two-thousand-year history of anti-Semitism. Such is the primitive "logic" and powerful emotion of a cultural complex.

Tom Kirsch has been attuned to this deeply painful cultural complex all his life, not just from his father's experience but also from his mother's. She was German, Jewish, and Jungian as well. Having lived the early history of the Jungian tradition so intimately, Kirsch has pursued an interest in the history of the early psychoanalytic movement as a whole and has worked "cross-culturally" with many Freudians over the years to develop a better sense of the seminal ideas, founding personalities, and social context of its origins. His work led to an invitation to speak at the recent History of Psychoanalysis Conference in Versailles, France. Keenly sensitive to the easily provoked historical animosity between Jungians and Freudians, he tailored his remarks to this primarily Freudian group in the most careful and least inflammatory way possible. He did not go looking to activate the primal split, but to promote mutual understanding and consideration of a shared early history.[13]

Shortly after Kirsch's remarks and a few friendly questions, a Freudian analyst in the back of the audience rose and said: "Look—there is an elephant in the room. Jung was an anti-Semitic Nazi. He was indirectly responsible for the death of relatives of people sitting in this room. How can we go on talking about the theoretical?" Kirsch, shaking almost as if a bomb had been dropped in the room, reacted by telling his personal story. He related his parents' experience as both German Jews and early students of Jung. But the "elephant in the room" was even bigger than what was being discussed.

If possible, its scale was even more monumental than the Holocaust and the question of Jung's anti-Semitism. The cultural complex triggered was the accumulated two-millennia history of the persecution of Jews, originating in the belief that the Jews were "Christ-killers." Naturally, it swallowed any further meaningful dialogue at the History Conference in an instant. Daimones beget Daimones, and the defenses of the collective spirit in both Freudians and Jungians remain the most potent force preventing significant dialogue about the history of psychoanalysis or a real rapprochement between Jungians and Freudians. The cultural complex and its archetypal defenses of the collective spirit put Jungians and Freudians in "sea-borne ships" similar to those of the early Greeks in the "Hymn of the Kouretes" or the "crazy" Cuban-Americans who sailed to our shores. They protect Baby Zeus from Kronos, Elian Gonzales from Fidel Castro, Christians from Jews and Jews from Christians, Jungians from Freudians and Freudians from Jungians. It's an old story.

And other holy wars

A new chapter of this type of old story literally exploded into our collective consciousness on September 11, 2001. Although this chapter was written and submitted for publication in the first half of 2001, a most horrific Muslim/Christian/Jewish eruption of daimonic forces deserves a comment from the perspective of the theories advanced in this chapter. Radical Islamism and its terrorist agenda can be understood as the expression of archetypal defenses of the collective spirit, set off by the activation of a cultural complex with more than a thousand years of accumulated historical experience. From this point of view, Osama bin Laden and the Mujahideen are Daimones—human but terrifyingly impersonal incarnations of the archetypal defenses of the collective spirit. They are the avenging angels of the deeply and long-traumatized spirit of the Muslim world. As Daimones, they may well end up further wounding and torturing the very traumatized Muslim Self that they have set out to defend. In addition to the awful tragedy of inflicting further injury to the Muslim spirit that the Daimones seek to protect is the psychological fact that possession by a cultural complex automatically triggers its bipolar, reciprocal opposite, namely the response of the Western world. It is no accident that George Bush made an unconscious slip when he first referred to a "crusade" as the Western world's response to the World Trade Center and Pentagon bombings. His slip was our cultural complex's answer to the jihad and puts us right back into the world of Constantine's Sword. Of course, for much of the Muslim world, George Bush is the Daimon. When such forces are unleashed in the collective psyche of nations, we are in much the same situation that Jung observed in "Wotan" his 1936 essay about Nazi Germany:

> Archetypes are like riverbeds which dry up when the water deserts them, but which it can find again at any time. An archetype is like an old watercourse along which the water of life has flowed for centuries, digging a deep channel for itself. The longer it has flowed in this channel the more likely it is that sooner or later the water will return to its old bed. The life of the individual as a member of society and particularly as part of the State may be regulated like a canal, but the life of nations is a great rushing river which is utterly beyond human control ... Thus the life of nations rolls on unchecked, without guidance, unconscious of where it is going, like a rock crashing down the side of a hill, until it is stopped by an obstacle stronger than itself. Political events move from one impasse to the next, like a torrent caught in gullies, creeks and marshes. All human control comes to an end when the individual is caught up in a mass movement. Then the archetypes begin to function, as happens also in the lives of individuals when they are confronted with situations that cannot be dealt with in any of the familiar ways.[14]

The ancient, archetypal riverbed of rivalrous conflicts between the Christians, the Jews, and the Muslims is once again overflowing with a gushing torrent that threatens to flood the world.

The Islamist dream of creating a new "caliphate" is a geographic projection of a wish to restore a wounded collective Muslim spirit through the creation of an empire that transcends national boundaries. The traumatized Self of the Muslim world suffered centuries of humiliation at the hands of a rapidly expanding Western civilization that captured the scientific, technological, and materialistic initiative that once belonged to the Muslim world. But, by the most ironic of historical twists, the Muslim world—deeply wounded in its collective self image—ended up with the richest share of the world's oil that is the current fuel for the materialist advances of Western civilization. Cultural complexes beget cultural complexes. Where they land in the individual psyche defines an emerging challenge for the culturally attuned depth analyst.

Conclusion

We hold strange mirrors up to ourselves and to one another when we start to explore cultural complexes as part of our personal and historical development. Our cultural complexes get all mixed up, not only with our personal history and complexes but also with other cultural complexes as well. These intermingling complexes take strange twists and turns over a lifetime and generations, creating exotic permutations and combinations within ourselves and between us and others, creating what I have come to think of as "recombinant visionary mythologies." The story of John Walker Lindh, a young Catholic boy from Marin County, California, who converted to Islam, fought for the Taliban/al Qaeda in Afghanistan, was captured by US forces, convicted as a traitor, and spent years in a US prison is a compelling example of how personal and cultural complexes can get entangled in a "recombinant visionary mythology."

In the other relatively straightforward personal stories I have been telling, Jim Carroll, an Irish Catholic, spent his adolescence growing up in post-Holocaust Germany, while Tom Kirsch, a Jew born of German parents, spent his Jungian adolescence in Los Angeles. Both found themselves expending tremendous psychic energy sorting themselves out in relation to these cultural complexes—Kirsch as a Jewish Jungian, Carroll as a former Catholic priest wrestling with the Church's historical relationship to Jews. What a burden it must have been for Tom Kirsch as a child of German Jewish Jungians to sort out the question of whether he has indirectly betrayed his people and the memory of the Holocaust. What a burden for Jim Carroll to have realized that as a devoted Catholic he could be held responsible for the "Christ-killer" myth that has resulted in the Crusades, the Inquisition, and the Holocaust. If we do not sort through our cultural as well as personal complexes carefully, we end up—at a minimum in the unconscious—feeling responsible for, identified with, or traumatized by events that belong to our cultural complexes more than our personal complexes.

Failure to consider cultural complexes as part of the work of individuation puts a tremendous burden on both the personal and archetypal realms of the psyche. Placing such a burden on the personal and/or archetypal dimensions by ignoring the careful sorting out of cultural complexes does not allow for the freeing up of the tremendous energy held in the grip of cultural complexes and making it available for the development of healthier individuals, who are able to have positive interaction with group and cultural life. Too often the Jungian notion/bias of "differentiating out from the collective" in the service of individuation does not take into account either the role of cultural complexes in development or the need to make a place for oneself in the life of the group.

The young Kouretes or Daimones, leaping for godly Themis—the spirit of the community—have taken us on a rather circuitous journey from Baby Zeus to Elian Gonzales to Catholics and Jews, Jung and Freud, radical Muslims and the West. Collective emotion and its enthusiasm, in leaping for the communal spirit and securing its protection, not only guarantee the health of crops and cities but can also destroy many citizens and communities along the way. For those reasons, one is well advised to give equal consideration to the personal, the cultural, and the archetypal dimensions of our life experience when considering human value, history, and meaning.

Notes

1 Thomas Singer, "The Cultural Complex and Archetypal Defenses of the Collective Spirit: Baby Zeus, Elian Gonzales, Constantine's Sword, and Other Holy Wars," *The San Francisco Jung Institute Library Journal* 20, no. 4 (2002), 5–28, DOI: 10.1525/jung.1.2002.20.4.5. Reprinted by permission of C. G. Jung Institute of San Francisco, www.sfjung.org.

2 Jane Ellen Harrison, *Themis: A Study of the Social Origins of Greek Religion* (Cambridge, UK: Cambridge University Press, 1912), Internet Archive, at https://archive.org/details/themisstudyofsoc00harr/page/n8.

3 Ibid., 7–8.

4 Donald E. Kalsched, *The Inner World of Trauma: Archetypal Defenses of the Personal Spirit* (London: Routledge, 1996).

5 Thomas Singer, ed, *The Vision Thing; Myth, Politics and Psyche in the World* (London: Routledge, 2000).

6 Harrison, *Themis*, 7.

7 Joseph Henderson, *Cultural Attitudes in Psychological Perspective* (Toronto: Inner City Books, 1984).

8 Samuel Kimbles, "The Cultural Complex and The Myth of Invisibility," in *The Vision Thing: Myth, Politics and Psyche in the World*, ed. Thomas Singer, 157–169 (London: Routledge, 2000).

9 John Weir Perry, "Emotions and Object Relations," *Journal of Analytical Psychology* 15, no. 1 (1970): 1–12.

10 C. G. Jung, *Memories, Dreams, Reflections*, ed. Aniela Jaffé (New York: Vintage Books, 1989), 246f.

11 James Carroll, *Constantine's Sword: The Church and the Jews, A History* (Boston: Houghton Mifflin Company, 2001).

12 Ibid., 175.

13 Thomas B. Kirsch., "Reports on the VIIIth International Meeting of the International Association for the History of Psychoanalysis (IAHP)," *Journal of Analytical Psychology* 46, no. 3 (July 2001): 496–498.

14 C. G. Jung, "Wotan" (1936), *The Collected Works of C. G. Jung*, vol. 10, *Civilization in Transition* (Princeton: Princeton University Press, 1968), ¶395.

3 Unconscious forces shaping international conflicts

Archetypal defenses of the group spirit from revolutionary America to conflict in the Middle East

From *The San Francisco Jung Institute Library Journal* 25, no. 4 (2006).[1]

The notion of archetypal defenses of the group spirit continued to fascinate me and I elaborated it in a second article on the topic in 2006.

An aspect of the emerging theory of cultural complexes that continues to grip me is what I termed in an earlier essay the archetypal defenses of the group spirit.[2] This phrase is a mouthful, but its purpose is to offer a precise psychological description of a level of collective emotional life that is deeply responsive to threat—whether the threat is real or simply "perceived" as real. When this part of the collective psyche is activated, the most primitive psychological forces come alive for the purpose of defending the group and its collective spirit or Self. I capitalize *Self* because I want to make it clear that it is not just the persona or ego identity of the group that is under attack but something at an even deeper level of the collective psyche, which one might think of as the spiritual home or "god" of the group. The tendency to fall into the grips of an identification with an archetypal defense of the group spirit is universal, and almost every one of us has experienced such a "possession" at some time in our lives—at least in one if not many of the primary groups to which we belong simultaneously.

The tribal spirit of the clan or of the nation often lies dormant or in the background, but when it is threatened, the defenses mobilized to protect it are ferocious and impersonal. The mobilization of such potent, archaic defenses is fueled by raw collective emotion and rather simplistic, formulaic ideas and/or beliefs. One can think of the more virulent cultural complexes as being fed by a vast underground pool of the collective emotional life. Archetypal defenses of the group spirit are animated by the release of these heightened emotions of groups in distress.

Just as Jung first investigated personal complexes through their activation by trigger words such as *mother* or *father* in his word-association tests,[3] cultural complexes are also frequently triggered by a collective word-association process that takes on a life of its own in the psyche of the group and that can be manipulated by skillful political operatives who use specific trigger words to activate the primitive emotions that fuel cultural complexes. In our current international vocabulary of cultural complexes, *holy jihad* or *axis of evil* or *crusade* or *terror* come to mind as trigger words and phrases for the seemingly endless pool of global distress in the emotional life of groups, which seems to be cheaper and much more easily tapped than any other natural resource that fuels collective life. Once a certain level of emotional intensity is achieved in the psyche of the group, archetypal defenses of the group spirit come to the forefront and begin to determine and even dictate how the group will think, feel, react, and behave.

These activated archetypal defenses of the group spirit find concrete expression in forms as varied as the unrest of divided populations over the legal status of foreign immigrants in countries around the world, the threatened development of nuclear weapons by nation-states such as Iran or Korea, the deployment of suicide bombers by terrorist groups, or the launching of massive military expeditions by world powers. And these same kinds of archetypal defenses come alive in all sorts of skirmishes between diverse groups of people who are not necessarily armed with explosive devices but perceive themselves in a threatened or disadvantaged position in which their most sacred values are in jeopardy—LGBTs, African Americans, women, the Christian right in the United States, the Muslim Brotherhood throughout the Middle East. The list of groups threatened at the core of their being or at the level of the group Self seems endless. And archetypal defenses of the group spirit are as likely to emerge in local group conflicts as they are in international conflicts (Figure 3.1).

In this chapter, I want to gradually build on several examples of how the psychology of archetypal defenses of the group spirit expresses itself. The building blocks of this chapter's thesis include the creation of the American Revolutionary flag, the contemporary language of a presidential speech, two historical examples of such archetypal defenses in action, a modern opera, and finally a film, Stephen Spielberg's *Munich,* in which the various building blocks of the chapter's argument are most fully teased out. Flag, speech, political action, opera, and film are several of the natural forms in which the collective psyche finds symbolic expression. First, however, I want to review some of the basic terms that are used to frame this inquiry: collective psyche, archetypal defenses, and group spirit.

Figure 3.1 Bloods and Crips. Rival groups—whether it be the Bloods and Crips or the Jungians and Freudians—can easily fall into conflicts in which the predominant exchange is between their archetypal defenses of the group spirit, which can carry arms in many forms—from guns to laws to propaganda to cartoons. (Jake Messing, by permission. Mixed media painting, 14 × 22 in, from the *Martyrs* series, which can be viewed at www.jakemessing.com.)
(https://aras.org/vision-reality-complex)

Collective psyche

Observations of group life in the Jungian tradition have led to the notion that there is a collective psyche that is far more than the sum of the individual psyches of those who belong to the group.[4] The more positive side of this notion is familiar to anybody who has participated in a team sport, who will know that the quality of play has as much to do with the collective psyche of the team as it does with the skills and flaws of the team's individual members. And, on the more negative side, anybody who has been in a crowd or an organization that begins to lose control of its emotional life knows how frightening, unruly, and destructive the collective psyche can become.

Even when not in the grips of cultural complexes, the collective psyche tends to "think" and "feel" in simplistic ways. When aroused, the collective psyche behaves much more like a beast than a rational being. The beast of the collective psyche is prone to simplistic thinking, abrupt emotional swings, and crude behavior. Rarely does the beast of the collective psyche engage in what we tend to value most in psychology and social life—differentiated dialogue and exchange. Of course, the collective psyche can be mobilized to effective action when rallied around a core belief or deep fear. More often than not, however, the collective psyche is primitive, nonrational, simplistic, easily manipulated, and stirred into an emotional frenzy with trigger words and images. When I think of the simple stimulus/response of a group's reaction to threat or injury, I see single-celled organisms such as an amoeba under the microscope— recoiling and secreting toxins to defend against alien stimulation. Other metaphors to describe the collective psyche include the simple reflexes elicited in a neurological exam or the inflammation and fever caused by viral or bacterial infections. It may well turn out that using the language of biology to describe the collective psyche in its primitive reflexes, inflamed eruptions, and delirious fevers may be far more than metaphoric. In time, the relatively new science of neuroimaging could uncover a biological substrate or "wiring" for the psychology of the collective psyche in the human brain. Indeed, there could even be a biological basis for the psychology of the particular type of group behavior I am describing in this chapter—the archetypal defenses of the group spirit.

Group spirit

As I formulate it, the group spirit is akin to what we Jungians might call the "Self" of the group. The *group spirit* is comprised of the ineffable core beliefs or sense of identity that bind people together. Sports teams have a group spirit and their fans often magically participate in it. Nation-states have a group spirit and their citizens often magically and unconsciously participate in it—particularly in times of crisis. Religious faiths have a group spirit, often symbolized by a part human/part divine being. Ethnic groups, gender groups, and racial groups all have a group spirit that is frequently felt and identified with in a myriad of ways. The group spirit can be symbolized by animals, humans, inanimate objects, and, in its most ineffable form, the refusal to symbolize it in imagery at all. The group spirit has many different elements that have come together in a seamless, often wordless, and even imageless, nonmaterial whole that is known to its members through a sense of belonging, shared essential beliefs, core historical experiences of loss and revelation, deepest yearnings, and ideals. One can begin to circle around the nature of a group's spirit by asking questions such as:

What is most sacred to the group?

What does the group treasure most?

What binds the group's members together?

Donald Kalsched's writings about the psychodynamics of the "personal spirit" can easily be extended to a description of the group spirit:

Occasionally it appears as a special animal—a favorite pet, a kitten, puppy or bird. Whatever its particular incarnation, this "innocent" remainder of the whole self seems to represent a core of the individual's imperishable personal spirit—what the ancient Egyptians called the "Ba-soul," or Alchemy, the winged animating spirit of the transformation process, i.e. Hermes, Mercurius. This spirit has always been a mystery—an essence of selfhood never to be fully comprehended. It is the imperishable essence of the personality—what Winnicott referred to as the "True Self" and which Jung, seeking a construct that would honor its transpersonal origins, called the Self.[5]

What makes the psychology of individuals in relation to the group spirit far more complex is that any one individual can belong to multiple groups simultaneously and feel a deep connection to the group spirit of more than one group at a time—even when two groups or more that an individual belongs to are in direct conflict with one another. We can all imagine that our "personal spirit" has affinities to more than one "group spirit" at a time. Such conflicting loyalties can occur around racial, ethnic, religious, and national identities.

Archetypal defenses of the group spirit

Donald Kalsched postulated that, in response to severe trauma, an individual develops defenses of the personal spirit.[6] I suggest that groups react in much the same way: when a group has been attacked at the core of its being and values—as the United States was on 9/11—or when a group has been corroded at the core of its being and values—as Islam has been for the past five hundred years—archetypal defenses are mobilized to protect the vulnerable and injured group spirit. These *archetypal* or *daemonic defenses* are ferocious and inhuman. The daemonic defenses often direct their primitive aggression back onto the wounded spirit of the group as evidenced in the self-mockery and self-denigration entrenched in the humor and self-perception of any number of oppressed minorities. But just as often these same defenses of the group spirit can turn their savage aggression out onto whomever or whatever appears to be a threat to the spirit, basic value, or identity of the group. I see this response as automatic, reflexive, and in some ways the most natural way for the group psyche to react. Those individuals identifying with the archetypal defenses of the group spirit can torture people in prison, behead people, and blow themselves and others up—without regard for their own personal well-being or the humanity of those who happen to be in their path. As defensive agents of a wounded group spirit, they are not constrained by normal human values or concerns. They are truly impersonal representatives of the group and its wounded spirit.

Although he was writing about the appearance of archetypal defenses or "defenses of the self" in the life of the individual infant, Michael Fordham's formulation of the nature of archetypal defenses can apply just as easily to the appearance of these defenses in the life, even in the infancy, of the group psyche and its individual members:

A persistent overreaction of the defense-system may start to take place; (attacks on not-self objects) may become compounded with parts of the self by projective identification, so that a kind of auto-immune reaction sets in; this in particular would account for the *persistence*

of the defense after the noxious stimulation had been withdrawn
[emphasis added] ... little or no inner world can develop; the self-integrate becomes rigid and persists... all later developments based
on maturational pressures result not in deintegration but disintegration
and the predominance of defense systems leads to the accumulation of
violence and hostility, which is split off from any libidinal and loving
communication with the object that may take place.[7]

Fordham's developmental approach to the origins of archetypal defenses of
the Self raises another interesting possibility with regard to the emergence
of archetypal defenses in group life. One can speculate that the time of
onset, severity, and duration of trauma in the group's developmental history
will contribute to the formation of its "Self" and its archetypal defenses.
If severe, long-lasting trauma has been at the core of the group's earliest
development, one can imagine that its defenses will tend to be most primitive and rigid. The corollary would be that the more developed and mature
the group "Self" has had a chance to become without crippling trauma, the
more likely it is for there to be some flexibility in its defensive structure.
And the more beaten down and wounded a group has been over time with
the accumulation of multiple traumas in its history, the more likely it is that
its archetypal defenses will be less responsive to rational intervention.

Don't tread on me: 1775

I would now like to give a series of examples of how the collective psyche,
group spirit, and archetypal defenses interact in a dynamic psychological
process. What makes this first example so interesting is that the voice of the
collective psyche found expression in a symbol in which the group spirit
and its archetypal defenses are actually one and the same. In later examples,
there is a more easily discerned distinction between the spirit of the group
and the defenses that are mobilized to protect it when it is attacked.

This symbolic expression (Figure 3.2) of the collective psyche first
appeared in the mid-1770s during the American Revolutionary period—in
the infancy of the American republic. Against a yellow background, the so-
called Gadsden flag features a rattlesnake coiled for attack that sits above
the defiant warning "Don't tread on me." About the symbol of the rattlesnake, a journalist (now thought by many scholars to have been none other
than Benjamin Franklin) wrote in the *Pennsylvania Journal:*

> The rattlesnake is found in no other quarter of the world besides
> America ... She never begins an attack, nor, when once engaged,
> ever surrenders: She is therefore an emblem of magnanimity and true

Figure 3.2 The Gadson flag (www.gadsden.info).
(https://aras.org/vision-reality-complex)

courage ... she never wounds 'till she has generously given notice, even to her enemy, and cautioned him against the danger of treading on her.

Franklin goes on to write:

I confess I was wholly at a loss what to make of the rattles, 'till I went back and counted them and found them just thirteen, exactly the number of the Colonies united in America; and I recollected too that this was the only part of the Snake which increased in numbers. ... 'Tis curious and amazing to observe how distinct and independent of each other the rattles of this animal are, and yet how firmly they are united together, so as never to be separated but by breaking them to pieces. One of those rattles singly, is incapable of producing sound, but the ringing of thirteen together is sufficient to alarm the boldest man living.[8]

If we interpret what Ben Franklin wrote in December 1775 about the coming together of the image of a rattlesnake and the motto, "Don't Tread on Me" in terms of collective psyche, archetypal defenses, and group spirit, the following conclusions seem apparent: the collective psyche of the times was caught by a revolutionary fervor in which the yearning for freedom (what I am calling "the group spirit") became identified with the defiant defense of "freedom" (what I am calling "the archetypal defense of the group spirit"). The image of the rattlesnake coupled with the words "Don't Tread on Me" fused the central value of the group with its ardent defense. One might even say that the archetypal defense of the group spirit first appeared in the infancy of our nation's development, much as was described by the Michael Fordham quote earlier in this chapter.

Ben Franklin saw the rattlesnake as "an emblem of magnanimity and true courage." I do not think that is how most people would describe the rattlesnake today. Franklin viewed the snake's nature as being positive. And, indeed, if the serpent's aggression were mobilized to protect the group Self—the about-to-be born sense of nationhood and freedom—one can imagine it would be seen as an ally. But, an archetypal defense of the group spirit is neither good nor bad—it simply is, and I would argue that in this first symbolic image of our country the rattlesnake represents a primal instinct of defensive aggressiveness at the group level of the psyche. Furthermore, there is something in all of us at the level of our group lives that can spring into reflexive, emotional action when triggered by a sense of danger—whether it is around issues of race, ethnicity, gender, nationality, or a host of other group identities and loyalties. For the sake of our group's survival, we can become like the rattlesnake—either the good rattlesnake of Ben Franklin or the paranoid, defensive rattlesnake of a more modern psyche—or we can be struck dumb in terror when we come across the rattlesnake in members of other groups—or we can be both at the same time. The symbol of the rattlesnake does suggest that any aggression requires a lethal response and seems to valorize a reflexive rather than reflective response to threat.

Freedom and archetypal defenses of the group spirit: A George Bush speech in 2005

There is a 250-year segue from the appearance of the "Don't Tread on Me" flag to George Bush's speech of December 14, 2005, on the eve of the historic vote for a Parliament in Iraq. But, in terms of the psychology we are exploring, the gap in time is of little consequence: the fundamental process underlying both events—the activation of archetypal defenses of the group spirit—remains the same. Just as the "Don't Tread on Me" rattlesnake became the symbol of the colonies' newly born freedom as well as the defense of that freedom, I want to point out how analogous archetypal defenses of the group spirit have shaped the text of George Bush's speech. The focus of this chapter is not on whether it was right or wrong to invade Iraq or, for that matter, right or wrong to begin the American Revolutionary War. Nor is it a question of whether archetypal defenses of the group spirit are good or bad. Rather, the questions I want to ask of George Bush's speech have to do with teasing out the ways in which the psychology of archetypal defenses of the group spirit has structured both George Bush's response to 9/11 and the American invasion of Iraq. In that context, consider the almost schematic logic of how this primitive group psychology works by looking at George Bush's statements regarding our nation's group spirit and its defense:

Core values of the American group spirit

In his speech, Bush identified our most sacred values as being centered on "the story of freedom" and "the principle that all men are created equal." He states explicitly that he believes our values are what is most desired and valued by the people of the Middle East.

> "We are living through a watershed moment in the story of freedom. Our efforts to advance freedom in Iraq are driven by our vital interests and our deepest beliefs. America was founded on the principle that all

men are created equal. And we believe that the people of the Middle East desire freedom as much as we do."⁹

Attack on core values

In his speech, George Bush repeated his belief that 9/11 has inaugurated a new era in which what is most sacred to our nation and its spirit will be under ongoing attack.

"On September 11, 2001, our nation awoke to a sudden attack, and we accepted new responsibilities. We are confronting new dangers with firm resolve.

We saw the future the terrorists intend for our nation on that fateful morning of September 11, 2001. That day we learned that vast oceans and friendly neighbors are no longer enough to protect us."

Defense of core values through aggressive counterattack

Finally in this speech, President Bush asserts that the threat of ongoing attack justifies the mobilization of every defensive/aggressive action we can muster to protect our national spirit.

"We are hunting down the terrorists and their supporters. We will fight this war without wavering. We cannot allow the world's most dangerous men to get their hands on the world's most dangerous weapons. In an age of terrorism and weapons of mass destruction, if we wait for threats to fully materialize, we will have waited too long."

The "logic" of these arguments is very simple and easy to follow—to many so simplistic that it has become the source of derision by citizens in the United States and elsewhere. But it is a mistake to think that because the "logic" is so simple—like the reactions of a single-celled organism—that it is not effective or gripping at the level of the collective psyche. Indeed, this is the kind of "logic" that rouses the emotions of the collective psyche and stimulates the reflexive activation of the archetypal defenses of the group spirit. It is our modern-day rattlesnake with its very clear message: "Don't Tread on Me."

Dr. Atomic: The bomb as an incarnation of an archetypal defense of the group spirit

If the "Don't Tread on Me" flag provided a natural segue to George Bush's December 2005 speech justifying our aggressive defense of freedom in the

United States and the Middle East, George Bush's speech is itself a natural segue to my consideration of America's development of the atomic bomb in World War II. In terms of the thesis I am developing here, one could say that one archetypal defense of the group spirit begets the next archetypal defense of the group spirit. Consider again the following words from George Bush's speech:

> "We cannot allow the world's most dangerous men to get their hands on the world's most dangerous weapons. In an age of terrorism and weapons of mass destruction, if we wait for threats to fully materialize, we will have waited too long."[10]

Just sixty years before Bush uttered these words, the same sentiments were fueling the United States' feverish efforts to develop an atomic bomb. It was feared that Hitler and the Nazis—also "the world's most dangerous men"— were well on their way to developing a nuclear device of their own. In a very real sense, the scientists at Los Alamos believed they were engaged in a scientific race to save the human race, and the historical truth seems to be that their belief was justified by what was later learned about Hitler's efforts to develop an atomic device, which he planned to drop first on London. It is an objective fact of history that the development of the atomic bomb was a necessity, dictated by the very real threat that Hitler would be the first to create such a weapon.

Karlyn Ward's review of John Adam's opera *Dr. Atomic* in the *San Francisco Jung Institute Library Journal* offers an excellent psychological description and analysis of Robert Oppenheimer, the Manhattan project he led, and the awesome scientific, ethical, and religious conflicts associated with developing the first nuclear weapon.[11] The actual creation of the bomb in 1945 and the story that Adams tells about its creation are separated by sixty years. In the decades between the creation of the bomb and the opera about its creation, I would argue that the bomb has taken up residence in the collective psyche as an incarnation of an archetypal defense of the group spirit. The story of the bomb's birth is one of the most important narratives of our era because it chronicles the creation of a modern archetype, not just a weapon. The atomic bomb is the ultimate modern concretization of an archetypal defense of the group spirit. Such weapons are both absolutely real and absolutely symbolic. They serve as centerpieces of global military strategy and as centerpieces of global psychological, symbolic reality. The opening chorus of *Dr. Atomic* summarizes precisely this situation: the creation of the modern archetypal defense of the group spirit:

A weapon has been developed
that is potentially destructive
beyond the wildest nightmares
of the imagination;
a weapon so ideally suited
to sudden unannounced attack
that a country's major cities
might be destroyed overnight
by an ostensibly friendly power.
This weapon has been created
not by the devilish inspiration
of some warped genius
but by the arduous labor
of thousands of normal men and women
working for the safety of their country.[12]

The last lines of the chorus are central to our discussion. There are two essential points to be noted here:

1. "... the bomb is the creation of normal men and women"—or, the energies of the collective and its psyche have been harnessed to create an "archetypal defense."
2. "... working for the safety of their country"—or, in the language of our thesis, to protect the values, spirit, and very existence of their group. In other words, I think that Adams is not only telling the story of the actual building of the bomb, but his opening chorus is also telling us that the group spirit has been mobilized to create a defense of its Self.

Perhaps even more chilling and speaking directly to the issue of creating an archetypal defense of the group spirit are Oppenheimer's own words:

We waited until the blast had passed, walked out of the shelter and then it was extremely solemn. We knew the world would not be the same. A few people laughed, a few people cried. Most people were silent. I remembered the line from the Hindu scripture, the Bhagavad-Gita: Vishnu is trying to persuade the Prince that he should do his duty; and to impress him he takes on his multiarmed form and says, "Now I am become Death, the destroyer of worlds." I suppose we all thought that, one way or another.[13]

From this statement, it is clear that Oppenheimer was living close to— even in touch with—the archetypal realm. And, he wasn't just speaking for his psyche alone when he quoted Vishnu as saying, "Now I am become Death, the destroyer of worlds." He was speaking for the collective psyche of his group. I believe that Oppenheimer understood that he and all his coworkers had become—like Vishnu—the embodiment of an "archetypal defense" that could bring death and destroy worlds. Presumably every suicide bomber in Palestine and Iraq knows and even celebrates the same truth—that to defend what one believes to be most sacred, the very "spirit of the group," one may be called upon to "become Death." In that sense, an individual can identify with and become an agent of the archetypal defense of the group spirit.

Dr. *Atomic* and conflict in the Middle East

A fascinating link between Dr. Atomic and the current conflict in the Middle East (Syria, Iraq, Iran, Palestine, Israel, and so on) is that nuclear weapons often take center stage in both dramas. In the case of the opera, the bomb itself is the major character and literally occupies center stage throughout the production. In the Iraq War, the fear of the bomb became a major player. What makes the unfolding of these narratives so chilling is that in both cases the original motivation/rationale for building the bomb in World War II or for destroying the ability to make the bomb in Iraq became more or less irrelevant once the ventures were underway. As you recall, it was the race with the Germans to develop the bomb that precipitated the Manhattan project. But when the Germans surrendered, American work on the bomb's development continued despite the outraged protests of the younger scientists at Los Alamos. They felt that a legitimate rationale for building the bomb no longer existed with the collapse of Hitler. In the case of the Iraq War, the suspicion that Saddam Hussein was doing everything he could to obtain weapons of mass destruction was given as a primary reason for going to war. After launching the war, that "reason" vanished before the eyes of the international community, but the Bush administration continued to maintain that the war was right for other reasons, such as the likely support of terrorists by the Hussein regime. This interesting parallel is worth exploring—that even though the original reasons for building the first nuclear device in 1945 and for launching the Iraq War dissolved, both projects had such deep psychological momentum that they still seemed essential and could not be stopped.

I would argue that this momentum was far more powerful than the rational reasons put forward for both ventures because of the existence of archetypal defenses of the group spirit. Once these psychological defenses of the collective psyche are mobilized for whatever reasons, the momentum for destructive, murderous activity on a grand scale is very hard to slow down or stop. In this regard, one is reminded of what Fordham wrote about the "*persistence of the defense after the noxious stimulation had been withdrawn.*"[14] Whether in the individual or group psyche, once such powerful defenses have been set in motion, they seem to have to run their course, which may well last far longer than the original precipitating threat, injury, or fear may seem to justify. For this reason, the reactions precipitated by these defenses can be likened to an autoimmune response in the body politic in which defenses proliferate and begin to take over a group. Domestic surveillance comes to mind as a contemporary American example in which the fear of terrorism and the desire to defend the country has led to increased spying on ourselves, which itself poses a threat to the very freedoms that lie at the core values of the group. Or, another sort of inflammatory, defensive proliferation was the increase of US nuclear weapons from 200 in 1950 to over 18,000 by 1960 as a reaction to the Soviet threat during the Cold War. Once set in motion, archetypal defenses of the group spirit seem to gain strength and momentum in a self-perpetuating emotional response in the group psyche—not unlike a "wave" that gets going at certain sporting events in which the crowd reaction reinforces and intensifies the crowd's enthusiasm and support for the "home team."

Another truly treacherous aspect of the dynamics of the archetypal defenses of the group spirit is their capacity to generate an isomorphic or reciprocal response in other groups. Bush's statement, "We cannot allow the world's most dangerous men to get their hands on the world's most dangerous weapons," ends up getting turned on its head not just by Iran, but also by others who had not been seen as a threat by us. For instance, many Europeans, who are outside of our projective field of "terrorists," have seen Bush's shadow clearly in his own remarks and have come to regard the US government as composed of "the world's most dangerous men."

It has come as a great surprise to many Americans that the United States is seen as the world's greatest threat. What does a country do in the face of "the world's most dangerous men" and "who are the world's most dangerous men?" Here is what Jojjat-el-Eslam Mohssen Gharavian, a senior cleric and spiritual advisor to the current president of Iran, said about nuclear weapons and the United States in his Fatwa of February 15, 2006: "Whereas the entire world has nuclear arms, it is only natural that this form of weapon will be available to us for the purpose of a retaliatory strike against those aspiring to attack us with nuclear weapons."[15] The perplexing, contemporary geopolitical logic of who gets to possess the "Bomb" takes us full circle to the "Don't Tread on Me" flag, whose motto of defiance is now ironically being shouted at the United States by Iranians. In his *New York Times* Op-Ed piece, a scholar of Persian history, Abbas Amanat, notes: "Painful collective memories have made Iran's pursuit of nuclear energy a national symbol of defiance that has transcended the motives of the current Islamic regime."[16]

Earlier in the essay, I pointed out how the "group spirit" of freedom in the American Revolutionary flag was conflated with its archetypal defense in that symbolic expression. There are many who think that the creation of the Atomic Bomb has led America back to that original state of being, that is, we have allowed the spirit of who we are to get too identified with the defense of who we are. In the contemporary version of that conflation, the possession of ultimate weaponry exists not only for the defense of who we are, but itself has become one with who we are. E. L. Doctorow argues this most convincingly when he writes:

> We have had the bomb on our minds since 1945. It was first our weaponry and then our diplomacy, and now it's our economy. How can we suppose that something so monstrously powerful would not, after forty years, compose our identity? The great golem we have made against our enemies is our culture, our bomb culture—its logic, its faith, its vision.[17]

Doctorow might be saying: what started as a legitimate weapon based on historical necessity has transformed itself in our collective psyche into a symbol and archetypal defense with which we have become unconsciously identified. Doctorow's argument is that America itself has become what Oppenheimer feared in himself when he quoted Vishnu: "Now I am become Death, the destroyer of worlds." As America has edged toward "becoming Death, the Destroyer of Worlds," it has found its mirror image in the Islamic suicide bombers whose actions proclaim: "We too love death—so you will never defeat us."

Although the creation of the atomic bomb and the current war in Iraq have been separated in time by sixty years, they are linked by the fact that both have required the vast mobilization of human and material resources. And, in both cases, this has been justified by the argument that the very future of Western civilization has been at stake. Such a threat in the collective psyche leaves us all with the terrible dilemma of sorting out how to respond to this most primitive psychological defensive reaction in the group and in ourselves. A psychological fact is undeniable: the archetypal defenses of the American group spirit have been mobilized at the deepest level of the collective psyche by recent events around the world. Should the alarm that this induces (which is now actually color coded according to severity by the US government) be responded to as if the threat is real—or dismissed as politically induced hysteria or manipulation for other reasons? Did Hitler pose a real threat? Did Saddam Hussein pose a real threat? Does George Bush pose a real threat? Once the dread of these destructive forces, expressed on the faces of a country's leaders, is unleashed in the collective psyche, how do we evaluate them? Or do they demand that we reflexively defend our group because its very survival is at stake? These tormenting questions lead to the next example: Steven Spielberg's *Munich*.

Munich

Steven Spielberg's film *Munich* has stirred considerable controversy in its evocative retelling of the events surrounding the murder of eleven Israeli athletes by the Palestinian group Black September at the Munich Olympic games in 1972.[18] Once again, for the purposes of this chapter, I am going to examine certain aspects of the film primarily from the point of view of the collective psyche, the group spirit, and its archetypal defenses.

Viewing the film is a wrenching experience of the inexorable unfolding of a nightmare that will not stop. It is a nightmare that keeps adding to its own horror story—a waking nightmare of the implacable conflict between two groups of people that devours the individual lives of its citizens. It demonstrates two recurring themes that are the central concern of this chapter:

1. What happens when the group Self is attacked and its center becomes inflamed?
2. What happens at the affective/instinctual level of the personal psyche when the collective psyche is stirred up at its core?

Two lovemaking scenes, one near the beginning of the movie and one near the end of the movie, carry these central themes.

At the beginning of the movie, we are introduced to the drama of the Munich massacre in a collective way. We learn about the event as if we were watching television in 1972, and familiar American broadcasters of that era—Peter Jennings, Howard Cosell, Jim McKay—tell us what is happening. The mortified reactions of ordinary Israelis as they watch this on television show us that these Olympians are felt as the fathers, brothers, husbands, and sons of every Israeli family and that their murder is a profound wound and death threat to Israel's actual survival as well as its spirit. Equally true, witnessing the Palestinians' fascinated and emotional identification, as they watch the events unfold, shows us that the members of Black September are the avenging angels of a group whose spirit has been mauled for decades. The spirit of each group has been badly traumatized; the collective of each group has become inflamed at its core; and this inflammation expresses itself in the mobilization of a group response that is murderous, impersonal, primitive, and without individual human concern.

In a scene that is deeply moving for its subtle mix of personal and impersonal forces in human affairs, Golda Meir herself tells us what the Israelis are planning as a response to the Munich massacre. She issues a prophetic warning about what happens when the "collective" or "group psyche" awakens to such a nightmare: "Every civilization finds it necessary to make compromises with its own values." Or—we might translate—when the archetypal defenses of the group spirit are mobilized, the group may betray its own values in favor of what it believes is necessary for survival. In the case of Munich that means recruiting assassins to avenge the deaths of the slain Olympian athletes who have come to embody the "group spirit" of Israel.

After drawing us into its orbit by allowing us to participate in the collective view and reactions to Munich, the film gradually introduces us to the individual protagonists whose lives we will follow. Avner, the chief protagonist, is going home to his pregnant wife as he deliberates about whether to accept his new role as avenger of the group spirit. We observe him in bed, at the end of the first lovemaking scene with his wife, and the scene is tender, intimate, and very personal. The collective is about to shatter their early married life, but it has not yet entered Avner's lovemaking fantasies. What develops over the course of the film is that every time the protagonist gets close to his wife—every time he calls her or has some sort of contact with her, every time he has the hint of a personal life and a personal psyche—he (and we) are immediately brought back to the reality of the collective nightmare of Munich through a series of flashbacks in which the protagonist "sees" and "experiences" in his fantasies the details of what happened at Munich. In that sense, the collective events keep invading his individual psyche at the moments of his most personal and intimate experience. This increasing contamination and confusion of his individual psyche with the collective psyche is at the heart of the film, and I think it is at the heart of what happens when the personal and collective psyches in an individual begin to get infected with one another at the intersection of the group self and the personal spirit.

I think there is a psychological as well as dramatic genius to Spielberg's progressive use of the flashback sequences to show what happened in the Munich massacre. Dramatically, the viewer keeps circling around the unfolding horror of the events in Munich as they reveal themselves slowly in the hero's imagination over the course of the film. This allows the climactic events at Munich to parallel the psychological development of the film's main character. The murder at Munich and the character's fantasy life become one in the final lovemaking scene. The rhythm of the flashback sequences allows one to experience the gradual penetration of horror and rage into the psyche of the individual. Ultimately, I think it shows how the individual and the group have become one in Avner as his identity becomes that of assassin in his role as archetypal defender of the group spirit. It is at the affective and instinctual level of this merging that I think the film is most successful. Avner makes love in a trance, dazed and caught between two worlds. He is totally unrelated to his wife who witnesses his dissociation and says simply, "I love you." Rage, horror, fear, love, hate, sex, aggression, and profuse sweat play across his face in an emotional swirl in the reliving of the final moments of his compatriots at Munich. One wonders if this possession by the events and emotions of Munich are both the peak of the fever in Avner and the beginning of its lysis. Perhaps his sweat indicates a fever break in which the complete identification of his psyche with Munich is experienced to the core of his being, and, at the same time, the sweat marks the beginning of his disidentification with that possession. Afterward it does seem that Avner is no longer able to identify with being the avenging angel of the Israeli group spirit. He decides to remain in New York and breaks his unofficial but very real relationship with Mossad.

It is through this glimpse into Avner's emotional life that we get our best sense of what happens when archetypal defenses of the group spirit are activated in the psyche of the individual and the collective. Avner's agony in the final lovemaking scene gives us an almost microscopic view of the nature of the inflammatory process that takes hold of the emotional life of the individual and the group. In the grips of it, it is hard to imagine a cure, other than the fever running its course and breaking—loosening both the individual and the collective from its grip.

Conclusion

The threat of military attack is not the only way to arouse archetypal defenses of the group spirit (Figure 3.3). With mass media as the primary means of global communication, the recent wireless transmission of cartoons from one part of the world to another was sufficient to mobilize millions of people into a frenzy of protest about their sacred center being violated. Jokes, slurs, slogans, traumatic images such as photos of prison torture and humiliation—and a host of other weapons—can be used to provoke, prod, and agitate groups into a sense of being besieged and devalued. Indeed, almost every day newspapers seem to be reporting on some eruption of archetypal defenses of the group spirit of one group in relation to another. The phenomenon is ubiquitous, and the cure is elusive. Indeed, it is my opinion that these eruptions are inexorable, nonrational, and primitive.

Figure 3.3 An "axis of evil" is created when cultures and their complexes collide. This can happen anywhere—between the West and Islam on a global scale, between Israel and Palestine (as shown in *Munich,* between the Bloods and Crips in Los Angeles, or between two conflicting groups in a Jung Institute. The collage demonstrates in image form how a true "axis of evil" is created in a horrifying dance of destruction symbolized by the paired serpents of the archetypal defenses facing off against one another when the sacred spirits of the group are attacked—symbolized in this image by the crescent and the Mosque for Islam and by the candles of Western Christian and Jewish cultures. When core values are assaulted as in the 9/11 attack or aggression by Western troops in Islamic lands, the archetypal defenses of the conflicting groups, "headed" by the figures of bin Laden and Bush, generate the most terrible experience of mass and personal horror behind which lurks the ultimate symbol of modern destruction—the atomic bomb. Personal lives, cultural values, and archetypal forces collide and compete in the collective psyche. (Collage: Dyane Sherwood and Jacques Rutzky. All images but the last were taken from the internet. From top left: atomic bomb exploding; American bomb exploding in Iraq, 2003; bin Laden; Bush; 9/11 twin towers; Iraqi mosque; Gadsden rattlesnake; candles and flags placed in spontaneous memorial 9/11; Jihadists pose on internet video prior to beheading; US soldier threatens prisoner with dog at Abu Ghraib prison; medieval painting showing European Christians attacking a Muslim walled city.)

(https://aras.org/vision-reality-complex)

A careful analysis of a deeply entrenched, intractable cultural complex with its associated archetypal defenses of the group spirit might be thought of as equivalent to diagnosing an illness of the collective psyche. And, if we are able to diagnose the illness, we might then ask—what is the cure? We know at the individual level, one has to suffer a complex repeatedly until finally its toxic effects may be digested and transformed in some alchemy of the psyche. If that is the case, we might ask if Muslims, Jews, and Christians could learn to digest and transform their cultural complexes in some alchemy of the collective psyche. There seems to have been little real progress in such a process. In the United States, blacks and whites have been trying to digest and transform their interacting cultural complexes for 350 years. There has been some progress, but recent studies show that professed attitudes of tolerance are belied by tests designed to measure implicit attitudes.[19]

Still, one should try to imagine ways in which heated up cultural complexes and their archetypal defenses of the group spirit might be resolved. Do they get resolved simply by running their course like a fever—like McCarthyism did in the 1950s or perhaps neo-conservatism might in this decade? In that case, the cure is simply a matter of time, of waiting for the activated archetypal defenses of the group spirit to fall back into the cultural unconscious as they lose psychic energy.

Another way in which one might envision a cure or healing for these collective maladies is the occasional emergence on the scene of a charismatic leader who in his or her personhood carries the transcendent function for the collective psyche. It is as if there is a perfect fit between the experiences of a "chosen" individual that resonates with the experiences and needs of a group or even conflicting groups, pointing to a previously unimagined way to transcend roadblocks to resolution. Gandhi, Martin Luther King, Nelson Mandela, Desmond Tutu come to mind as being the kinds of leaders who embody a transcendent spirit for the collective psyche that leads to the vision of a real cure of cultural conflicts. Perhaps Barack Obama has the potential to embody in his being a transcendent function that might point to real reconciliation and healing of the entrenched cultural complexes that divide black and white communities in the United States. Another way of saying this is that some gifted individuals may have the capacity to experience in their psyches the cultural complexes that divide groups into warring factions and hold these cultural complexes in their psyches in such a way that an authentic experience of the transcendent comes alive in them. They must also have the ability to communicate this transcendent vision to the group.

In the meantime, most of us muddle along with the reality that many of these cultural conflicts are well beyond our efforts as individuals or as members of a group to find a cure. There is always the possibility that the "transcendent function" in the collective psyche can percolate up from "below"—that is, from everyday citizens who are moved to act for real healing in the social and political realm. In such a case, it is not a bold, visionary leader who embodies the transcendent function and leads the way, but something that bubbles up in the collective psyche that is carried simultaneously by many "average" people.

Notes

1 Thomas Singer, "Unconscious Forces Shaping International Conflicts: Archetypal Defenses of the Group Spirit from Revolutionary America to Confrontation in the Middle East," *The San Francisco Jung Institute Library Journal* 25, no. 4, (2006): 6–28, DOI: 10.1525/jung.1.2006.25.4.6. Reprinted by permission of C. G. Jung Institute of San Francisco, www.sfjung.org.

2 Thomas Singer, "The Cultural Complex and Archetypal Defenses of the Collective Spirit," *The San Francisco Jung Institute Library Journal* 20, no. 4 (2002): 5–28; Thomas Singer and Samuel Kimbles, eds., *The Cultural Complex: Contemporary Jungian Perspectives on Psyche and Society* (London and New York: Brunner-Routledge, 2004).

3   C. G. Jung, "Studies in Word Association" (1904–7, 1910), *The Collected Works of C. G. Jung*, vol. 2, *Experimental Researches* (Princeton: Princeton University Press, 1973).

4   For example, see C. G. Jung, *Civilization in Transition*, Bollingen Series XX (Princeton, Princeton University Press, 1975).

5   Donald E. Kalsched, *The Inner World of Trauma: Archetypal Defenses of the Personal Spirit* (London, Routledge, 1996).

6   Ibid.

7   Michael Fordham, "The Self and Autism," *Journal of Analytical Psychology* 33 (1976): 91.

8   Chris Whitten, Gadsen Info, at www.gadsden.info/history.html.

9   All quotes from the December 14, 2005, speech by President George Bush can be found at www.whitehouse.gov/news/releases/2005/12/20051214-1.html.

10 Ibid.

11 Karlyn Ward, "Batter My Heart …," *The San Francisco Jung Institute Library Journal* 25, no. 1 (2006): 51–77.

12 John Adams and Peter Sellars, unpublished libretto for Dr. Atomic.

13 Jennet Conant, *109 East Palace: Robert Oppenheimer and the Secret City of Los Angeles,* (New York: Simon and Schuster, 2005), 315–317.

14 Fordham, "The Self and Autism."

15 *DEBKAfile* 6, no. 243 (February 24, 2006).

16 Abbas Amanat, "The Persian Complex," *The New York Times,* May 25, 2006, A27

17 E. L. Doctorow, "We Have Had the Bomb" in "The State of Mind of the Union," *The Nation,* March 22, 1986, 330.

18 *Munich,* 2005. Screenplay by Tony Kushner and Eric Roth. Directed by Steven Spielberg.

19 M. R. Banaji & N. Dasgupta, "The Consciousness of Social Beliefs: A Program of Research on Stereotyping and Prejudice." In *Metacognition: Cognitive and Social Dimensions,* eds. V. Y. Yzerbyt, G. Lories, and B. Dardenne, 157–170 (London: Sage Publications, 1998); Bruce Bower, "The Bias Finders: A Test of Unconscious Attitudes Polarizes Psychologists," *Science News Online* 169, no. 16 (April 22, 2006). For those who want to test their own unconscious bias, a test can be taken online at https://implicit.harvard.edu/implicit/.

4 The cultural complex

A statement of the theory and its application

From *Psychotherapy and Politics International* 4, 2006.[1]

I was invited in 2006 to contribute an essay on cultural complexes to Psychotherapy and Politics International, a journal that offered the opportunity to reach a wider non-Jungian audience of psychotherapists interested in the interface of analytical psychology and politics. Although it repeats some of the background history, it represents a most concise and basic introduction to the theory of cultural complexes.

Since the fall of the Berlin Wall and the collapse of the binary worldview of conflicting global superpowers that it symbolized, an endless parade of ethnic, racial, religious, gender, national, and regional factions has emerged on the world stage with their long-simmering feuds bubbling over. Everywhere, disadvantaged and/or disenfranchised groups—whether representing a minority or a majority—have been crying out for justice, healing, or vengeance—or all three simultaneously. It seems as if peoples from every continent have been caught in a newly energized and endless round of conflicts that run the gamut from familial and tribal skirmishes to international hatreds. As these group conflicts flood relationships with highly charged emotions at every level of human exchange—from local to global—we seek explanations, understanding, and remedies. More often than not, such seeking leaves us feeling powerless in the face of the intractable nature of these feuds. Political theories, economic theories, sociological theories, religious theories, and psychological theories—all provide a partial glimpse of the truth as to what underlies and fuels these conflicts.

Over the past few years, I have been focusing on what I believe to be a core aspect of the psychological nature of conflicts between groups and cultures. This perspective is modeled on an old theory that I—along with my colleague and close collaborator Sam Kimbles—have been applying more systematically in a new arena: Jung's theory of complexes, which he developed at the beginning of the twentieth century. The modern version and new application of Jung's old idea makes no special claim to having the answer to what causes—or might heal—group and cultural conflict, but it offers a point of view that may be useful to some as they ponder the forces that invariably seem to thwart most human attempts to bring a peaceful, collaborative spirit to the unending strife between groups of people.

In our ripe time or "Kairos"—as Reinhold Niebuhr liked to call it—when understanding both the uniqueness and commonality of cultures from around the world has become essential for the well-being of the global community itself, shedding more light on what tears us apart is an essential first step. Much of what tears us apart can be understood as the manifestation of autonomous processes in the collective and individual psyche that organize themselves as cultural or group complexes. Cultural complexes are every bit as real, every bit as formative, every bit as ubiquitous, and every bit as powerful in their emotional and behavioral impact on individuals and groups as are personal complexes. Indeed, cultural complexes may present the most difficult and resistant psychological challenge we face in our individual and collective life today.

To tackle this most important problem of placing cultural complexes in context, I want to give the reader:

- A clear sense of what is meant by the notion of a "cultural complex"
- A clear sense of how the concept of a cultural complex is a natural and evolutionary development of C. G. Jung's very earliest psychiatric researches into the theory of complexes.[2]
- A simple sketch of a most virulent, contemporary example of a cultural complex.

Each "Part" of this chapter will present a step-by-step progression in which the building blocks of the concept and of the contemporary example are pieced together in a manner that shows how the concept of the cultural complex has been constructed and how it takes on living reality in the psyches of groups and of individuals.

Part one: The definition and theory of the "cultural complex"

There are two essential threads of Jungian theory that get woven into the fabric of our current thinking about cultural complexes:

- Jung's original theory of complexes
- Joseph Henderson's theory of the cultural unconscious

By weaving these two distinct threads together and then mixing in the threads of our contemporary perspectives and concerns, we have begun the work of extending complex theory into cultural life and conflicts.

Jung's original complex theory: Its relationship to individuation and the life of groups

Jung's first papers on the "Word Association Test" were published in 1902 and 1903. Out of those early experiments, based on timed responses to lists of words, was born Jung's idea of complexes. Interestingly, when the group that had formed around Jung in the 1930s was considering a name separate from the founder's, Jung himself thought it should be called "complex psychology." For many analytical psychologists, Jung's theory of complexes remains the cornerstone of the day-to-day work of psychotherapy and analysis. Like the Freudian theory of defenses, Jung's notion of complexes provides a tool for understanding the nature of intrapsychic and interpersonal conflict.

Through a hundred years of clinical experience, we have come to know well and accept that complexes are a powerful force in the lives of individuals. Most simply, we define a *complex* as an emotionally charged group of ideas and images that cluster around an archetypal core. Jung wrote:

> The complex has a sort of body, a certain amount of its own physiology. It can upset the stomach. It upsets the breathing, it disturbs the heart— in short, it behaves like a partial personality. For instance, when you want to say or do something and unfortunately a complex interferes with this intention, then you say or do something different from what you intended. You are simply interrupted, and your best intention gets upset by the complex, exactly as if you had been interfered with by a human being or by circumstances from outside.[3]

Today, we can say the same is true of a cultural complex when it possesses the psyche and soma of an individual or a group—it causes us to think and feel in ways that might be quite different from what we think we should feel or think, or, as Jung put it, "We say or do something different from what we intended." In other words, cultural complexes are not always "politically correct," although being "politically correct" might itself be a cultural complex.

The basic premise of our work, then, is that another level of complexes exists within the psyche of the group (and within the individual at the group level of their psyche). We call these group complexes *cultural complexes*, and they, too, can be defined as emotionally charged aggregates of ideas and images that tend to cluster around an archetypal core and are shared by individuals within an identified collective.

The theory and analysis of complexes, as worked out by analytical psychologists over the last century, has for the most part been applied to the psyche of individuals. Indeed, the goal of Jungian analysis in its individuation process has been to make one's personal complexes more conscious and free up the energy contained within them to be more available for creative psychological development. Elizabeth Osterman, a senior Jungian analyst of an earlier generation, liked to say that she had learned that her complexes would never completely disappear, but a lifetime of struggling with them had resulted in their debilitating effects, including foul moods, lasting only five minutes at a time rather than decades at a time. Some of the cultural complexes that we are exploring have caused uninterrupted foul moods in cultures for centuries, if not millennia, at a time (Figure 4.1).

Although Jung certainly included a "cultural level" in his schema of the psyche, his theory of complexes has never been systematically applied to the life of groups and to what Jung and his followers have been fond of calling the "collective."[4] I would say that the idea of a "cultural complex" is implicit in Jung's work, but he neither made it explicit, nor did

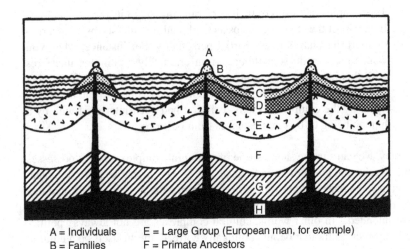

A = Individuals	E = Large Group (European man, for example)
B = Families	F = Primate Ancestors
C = Clans	G = Animal Ancestors in general
D = Nations	H = "Central Fire"

Figure 4.1 Jung's diagram of the psyche.
(https://aras.org/vision-reality-complex)

he systematically develop such an idea. Among other things, he didn't put forth the idea of a "cultural unconscious" in which to posit such "cultural complexes." It was Joseph Henderson's contribution to make the notion of a "cultural unconscious" explicit in the Jungian tradition. Many readers may already be protesting that Jung and Jungians have always had a keen interest in "the collective" and have actively explored diverse cultures, making enormous contributions to understanding the role of the "collective" in the psyche. Of course, this is true. But, when it came to understanding the psychopathology and emotional entanglements of groups, tribes, and nations, we maintain that Jung and Jungians have not taken full advantage of Jung's original theory of complexes and this has left a major gap in analytical psychology.

The Jungian attitude to "the collective"

To understand collective psychology, Jung had an uncanny knack of going straight to the archetypal level of the psyche—often quite compellingly. For example, in his seminal 1936 essay "Wotan," Jung warns of the primitive, mercurial god of lightning and destruction that was seizing the German psyche.[5] But by leaving the social, economic, and political level of the German psychological experience out of his analysis in "Wotan," Jung opened himself up to profound misunderstanding and misinterpretation. Had he included a more careful analysis of the historical and cultural aspects of the German experience and perhaps been able to frame it in terms of the activation of a cultural complex in the German psyche, he may not have been subject to the accusations of anti-Semitism and intoxication with "Wotan" that naturally attached itself to him and his essay.

In the Jungian tradition, the theory of the complex with its archetypal core has been the foundation for understanding and analyzing individuals. But when it has come to understanding and analyzing broader collective experience, analytical psychologists have relied on the theory of archetypes. Archetypal possession of the collective psyche is an all too real and dangerous psychic phenomenon, but there are a host of potent group phenomena (which seize the individual as well) that may be more fruitfully and accurately explored by thinking first in terms of cultural complexes and then perhaps moving to the archetypal level. This may also help avoid our tendency to archetypal reductionism that Jungian interpretations of group phenomena frequently suggest.

As stated, Jung was intensely curious about the differences between groups of people and their varying cultures. He was keenly attuned to what we now call the *cultural unconscious* or the *cultural level of the psyche*. He traveled to the Americas, to Africa, to Asia, and he was constantly exploring the sacred traditions and mores of other peoples. Certainly, Jung and his followers have taken careful note of different cultural types, which is evident, for example, in Jung's discussion of national personality characteristics.[6] On the other hand, Jung was so suspicious of the life of groups and the danger of archetypal possession in collective life that he tended to divorce the development of the individual through the individuation process from the individual's life in groups.

Clearly, a substantial part of Jung's genius was his sensitivity to the perils of the individual's falling into the grips of collective life. Like all who lived through the twentieth century, Jung witnessed the terrible side of collectivity. Beginning with the deadening effect of collective religious life on his father's spirit, Jung went on in October 1913—just prior to the Great War—to have vivid anticipatory visions of Europe suffering massive destruction, which he later reported as follows: "I realized that a frightful catastrophe was in progress, towns and people were destroyed, and the wrecks and dead bodies were tossing about on the water. Then the whole sea turned to blood."[7] In the later part of his life, he shared in the nightmare horror of imagining nuclear holocaust. It is easy to see why Jung had such a dread of the individual and group psyche falling into possession by collective and archetypal forces.

For these very good reasons, collective life more often than not has fallen into the Jungian shadow—so much so that it is easy to feel within the Jungian tradition as if the life of the group and the individual's participation in it exists in a no man's land, suspended in the ether somewhere between the much more important and meaningful individual and/or archetypal realms. This tendency for collective life to fall into the Jungian shadow has done a great disservice to the tradition of analytical psychology and its potential to contribute to a better understanding of group forces in the psyche.

Jung's natural introversion (and his appeal to other introverts) and his fundamental focus on individuation had an unacknowledged tendency to set the individual up against or in opposition to the life of the group. In the Jungian tradition (as in the more general Western tradition), the individual has been given the heroic task of slaying the group's devouring hold on him or her. Individuation and wholehearted participation in the life of the group do not fit together easily or naturally. There is something in the tension between the individual and the group that is wholesome and natural, but the Jungian tradition has magnified that tension beyond perhaps what is healthy for either the individual or the group. Maybe this is, in fact, a "cultural complex" of the Jungian tradition. Whether that is true or not, it is our hope that the notion of a "cultural complex" will lead to an enhanced capacity to see the shadow of the group in its cultural complexes more objectively, rather than the Jungian tendency to see the group itself as the shadow.

We may even begin to become more aware of the positive value of living in the "collective." We may also begin to get better at differentiating cultural complexes from individual complexes. The point I want to make here, however, is that, although Jung and the analytical psychologists he trained spoke at length about the nature of the collective psyche, including discussions of different national, ethnic, and religious characteristics, Jung's theory of complexes was never systematically extended beyond its fundamental relevance in the development of individual psychology to include its application to group life or the study of how complexes shape collective experience. Complexes clustered around archetypal cores have been at the heart of our understanding of the individual psyche but only peripheral to our study of the collective psyche. A Jungian psychology of group complexes as distinct from, independent of, and yet interrelated with, personal complexes has not been elaborated. For this reason, our psychology has tended to collapse group experience between the archetypal and personal poles.

Joseph Henderson's theory of the cultural unconscious

Just as a level of group or cultural complexes was more implicit than explicit in Jung's psychology, so, too, the level of a cultural unconscious was more implicit than explicit in Jung's model of the psyche until Joseph Henderson really pointed to its separate sphere of influence. In his paper on "The Cultural Unconscious," Henderson defined the cultural unconscious as

> an area of historical memory that lies between the collective unconscious and the manifest pattern of the culture. It may include both these modalities, conscious and unconscious, but it has some kind of identity arising from the archetypes of the collective unconscious, which assists in the formation of myth and ritual and also promotes the process of development in individuals.[8]

Over a period of several decades, Joseph Henderson introduced the notion of a *cultural level* of the psyche that he called "the cultural unconscious." He posited this realm as existing between the personal and collective unconscious. He further elaborated this idea in his book *Cultural Attitudes in Psychological Perspective*.[9] To many Jungians, Henderson's work opened the theoretical door on that vast realm of human experience that inhabits the psychic space between our most personal and our most archetypal levels of being in the world. Henderson's elaboration of the cultural level of the psyche has made greater space for the outer world of group life to find a home in the inner Jungian world and allowed those immersed in the Jungian inner world to recognize more fully the deep value the psyche actually accords to the outer world of collective cultural experience. However, the potential role of Jung's complex theory remained undeveloped in Henderson's discussions of the cultural unconscious. Extending Jung's theory of complexes into the territory of the "cultural level of the psyche," as first described by Joseph Henderson, is the work that Sam Kimbles and I have been addressing. We feel that it helps to specify how the cultural unconscious impinges on the psyche of individuals and groups through the development, transmission, and manifestation of cultural complexes.[10]

The theory of cultural complexes: Jung's theory of complexes and Henderson's theory of the cultural unconscious

It is time to assemble the building blocks of Jung's theory of "complexes" with Henderson's theory of the "cultural unconscious" and make the "cultural complex" addition to the ramshackle theoretical framework of analytical psychology. As personal complexes emerge out of the level of the personal unconscious in its interaction with deeper levels of the psyche, cultural complexes can be thought of as arising out of the cultural unconscious in its interaction with both the archetypal and personal realms of the psyche and with the broader outer world arena of schools, work and religious communities, media, and all the other forms of group life.

Characteristics of cultural complexes

Personal complexes and cultural complexes are not the same, although they can get all mixed up with one another. We suggest that personal and cultural complexes share the following characteristics.

- They express themselves in powerful moods and repetitive behaviors. Highly charged emotional or affective reactivity is their calling card.
- They resist our most heroic efforts at consciousness and remain, for the most part, unconscious.
- They accumulate experiences that validate their point of view and create a storehouse of self-affirming, ancestral memories.
- Personal and cultural complexes function in an involuntary, autonomous fashion and tend to affirm a simplistic point of view that replaces more everyday ambiguity and uncertainty with fixed, often self-righteous attitudes to the world.
- In addition, personal and cultural complexes both have archetypal cores; that is, they express typically human attitudes and are rooted in primordial ideas about what is meaningful, making them very hard to resist, reflect upon, and discriminate.

Attending to the personal, cultural, and archetypal levels of complexes requires respect for each of these realms without condensing or telescoping one into the other, as if one realm were more real, true, or fundamental than another. Cultural complexes are based on repetitive, historical experiences that have taken root in the collective psyche of a group and in the psyches of the individual members of a group, and they express archetypal values for the group. As such, cultural complexes can be thought of as the fundamental building blocks of an inner sociology. But this inner sociology does not claim to be objective or scientific in its description of different groups and classes of people. Rather, it is a description of groups and classes of people as filtered through the psyches of generations of ancestors. It contains an abundance of information and misinformation about the structures of societies—a truly inner sociology—and its essential components are cultural complexes.

Cultural complexes/cultural identity/national character

It is important to understand that "cultural complexes" are not the same as either "cultural identity" and/or what Jung called "national character," although there are times when cultural complexes, cultural identity, and national character can seem impossibly intertwined. For instance, those groups emerging out of long periods of oppression through political and economic struggle must define new identities for themselves that are often based on long-submerged traditions. This struggle for a new group identity can get all mixed up with underlying potent cultural complexes that have accrued experience and memory over centuries of trauma and lie slumbering in the cultural unconscious, waiting to be awakened by the trigger of new trauma. In the fierce and legitimate protest for a group identity freed up from the shackles of oppression, it is very easy for groups and individuals within the groups to get caught up in cultural complexes. And for some people, their complexes—cultural and personal—are their identity. But, for many others, there is a healthy cultural identity (or "cultural ego") that can clearly be seen as separate from the more negative and contaminating aspects of cultural complexes. Jung was getting at the idea of a cultural identity in his discussion of national character, but that notion took an ugly and controversial turn when the discussion of national character got confused with the controversy around Jung and anti-Semitism. One can see Jung struggling with this controversy in his March 2, 1934, letter to A. Pupato:

> The question I broached regarding the peculiarities of Jewish psychology does not presuppose any intention on my part to depreciate Jews, but is merely an attempt to single out and formulate the mental

idiosyncrasies that distinguish Jews from other people. No sensible person will deny that such differences exist, any more than he will deny that there are essential differences in the mental attitude of Germans and Frenchmen. ... Again, nobody with any experience of the world will deny that the psychology of an American differs in a characteristic and unmistakable way from that of an Englishman. To point out this difference cannot possibly, in my humble opinion, be in itself an insult to the Jews so long as one refrains from value judgments. If anyone seeking to pin down my peculiarities should remark that this or that is specifically Swiss, or peasant-like, or Christian, I just wouldn't know what I should get peeved about, and I would be able to admit such differences without turning a hair. I have never understood why, for instance, a Chinese should be insulted when a European asserts that the Chinese mentality differs from the European mentality ...[11]

In this letter, Jung's rather hurt tone and his feeling of being misunderstood suggests that the topic of national character itself became contaminated by the swirling emotionalism activated by a cultural complex. These same cultural complexes can lead to fascism, racism, and all of the other horrors committed in the name of perceived differences between groups of peoples. So it is important in defining cultural complexes to differentiate them from cultural identity and national character.

The bipolarity of cultural complexes

Another way to make this most important distinction between cultural complex and cultural identity and/or national character is to use the idea of the "bipolar complex" that John Perry introduced in his seminal paper on complexes in the individual psyche.[12] Perry spoke of the everyday ego as being quite different from the ego that has been taken over by a complex. When a complex is activated in the unconscious (for instance, rebellious son and authoritarian father), one-half of its bipolar content with its potent affect and one-sided perceptions of the world takes hold of the everyday ego and creates what Perry called "the affect-ego." The other part of the bipolar pair is projected out onto the person with whom one is caught in the complex, and they, in turn, become what Perry labeled an "affect-object." Hence, you get the ragged and highly charged interactions between an "affect-ego" and an "affect-object." Neither party in this unholy pair usually fares very well. This same notion of "affect-ego" and "affect-object" can be carried over into our discussion of cultural complexes to help make the distinction between cultural identity and cultural complex clearer. An individual or group with a unique cultural identity that is not in the grips of a cultural complex is much freer to interact in the world of people from other groups without being prey to the highly charged emotional contents that can quickly alter the perception and behavior of different groups in relation to one another. Once the cultural complex is activated in an individual or a group, however, the everyday cultural identity can be overtaken by the affect of the cultural complex. At that point, the individual and/or the group has entered the territory of what Perry called "affect-ego" and "affect-object"—but at the level of the cultural complex rather than personal complex.

Part two: An example of a cultural complex

Archetypes, cultural complexes, and riverbeds

In "Wotan," Jung's 1936 essay about Nazi Germany, he wrote:

> Archetypes are like riverbeds which dry up when the water deserts them, but which it can find again at any time. An archetype is like an old watercourse along which the water of life has flowed for centuries, digging a deep channel for itself. The longer it has flowed in this channel the more likely it is that sooner or later the water will return to its old bed. The life of the individual as a member of society and particularly as part of the State may be regulated like a canal, but the life of nations is a great rushing river which is utterly beyond human control ... Thus the life of nations rolls on unchecked, without guidance, unconscious of where it is going, like a rock crashing down the side of a hill, until it is stopped by an obstacle stronger than itself. Political events move from one impasse to the next, like a torrent caught in gullies, creeks and marshes. All human control comes to an end when the individual is caught up in a mass movement. Then the archetypes begin to function, as happens also in the lives of individuals when they are confronted with situations that cannot be dealt with in any of the familiar ways.[13]

Clearly, what Jung wrote in 1936 resonates with our current crisis between Islam and the West. The ancient archetypal riverbed of rivalrous conflicts between Christians, Jews, and Muslims is once again overflowing with a rushing torrent that threatens to flood the world. This is at the archetypal level. Can we say something about this same situation from the perspective of the notion of a cultural complex?

Cultural complexes can have very long histories, very long memories, and very powerful emotions embedded in them. Cultural complexes can both enshrine and encrust themselves in the consciousness and unconscious of groups of people, and they can intertwine themselves with the cultural complexes of other groups of peoples. Indeed, these intertwining and affect-laden energies of conflicting unconscious cultural complexes can form the pre-conditions for human events to unfold with a fury that can be likened to the natural forces portrayed in a movie of a few years ago called *The Perfect Storm*—when all of the climatic conditions off the eastern seaboard of the United States were uniquely positioned to come together and cause a storm of huge proportions. It is no stretch of the geopolitical, psychological, and spiritual imagination to say that we are living in a time when a rare config-uration of swirling cultural complexes have been aligning in just the right combination to unleash massive destructive forces.

The best way to know that one is touching a cultural complex—in either a group or an individual—is by the emotional reactivity that certain topics automatically trigger. Of course, this is how Jung first came to identify personal complexes—the emotional reactivity of a trigger word caused a significant delay in a timed response. And, today, exactly the same thing can be said about a cultural complex. A hallmark of a cultural complex is the emotional reactivity of trigger words, such as *George Bush* or *Osama bin Laden* or *war on terror* or *holy jihad* or *colonial empire*. I suspect that just about every reader has definite opinions and potent affects about these particular trigger words. I might venture to say that at least some of those strong opinions and potent affects belong to cultural complexes.

In writing this chapter, I debated with myself about whether I wanted to risk stepping on the emotional landmines of the virulent cultural complexes currently seizing Islam and the West. Is it possible to have an objective dialogue about the Iraq War, the War on Terror, or 9/11? Can we begin a psychological discussion about the conflict between the West and Islam by using the concept of the cultural complex as a vehicle for exploring the powerful affects, dogmatic ideas, and violent actions that are taking hold of people around the world? Is it possible to evoke something of the swirling forces at play at the level of the cultural unconscious in such a way as to shed light rather than just heat on the topic?

1492

In the course of my thinking about Islam and the West in preparation for a talk at the 2004 International Jungian Congress in Barcelona, a very spe-cific date in Spanish and world history sprang to mind—a date that can simultaneously be seen as the middle, the end, and the beginning of sev-eral interconnecting cultural complexes that we are currently in the grips of. This is not just a historical date—rather it should be thought of as

Figure 4.2 Muslim vs. European expansion, 1000–1700 CE.
(https://aras.org/vision-reality-complex)

locating in time and space a real embodiment of several profound symbolic movements in the collective psyche that have taken shape in the form of cultural complexes (Figure 4.2).[14]

The year 1492 marks the expulsion of the Moors *and* the Jews from Spain and the end of the Islamic presence and dominance in this part of Europe. The year 1492 also marks the discovery of the Americas by Spanish ships under Christopher Columbus (although this date does not stand out as a landmark of either discovery or celebration in the cultural consciousness or cultural complexes of contemporary American Indians).

What fascinates me about this map is that 1492 can also be seen as a watershed date that marks both the beginning of rise of the West and the beginning of the decline of Islam—a parallel and contrary movement that has been going on for at least the past five hundred years and the swirling affects and effects of which threaten to engulf us today. The bipolarity of this movement is obvious, compelling, and quite characteristic of how cultural complexes work—that is, of how two groups get caught in the conflicting, opposite, and spiraling movements of cultural complexes. If one looks at the geography of the unfolding of these conflicting cultural complexes, it is clear that Islam expanded mostly by land and the West leapfrogged around the world by sea. In taking the sea route, the West encircled the globe. In taking the land route, Islam seemed to be landlocked and outflanked. Looking at what we might think of as "cultural complex weather maps" of the West and Islam, first the one from 1492 and then comparing it to one from some 750 CE—some 750 years earlier—(Figure 4.3), we can see Islam's initial spread by land to dominance of the known world. Islam's rise was lightning quick, just about total, and marked almost exclusively by uninterrupted triumph. But by 1492 that movement had begun to reverse itself as the Islamic world began to shrink, a process that continued for the next several centuries. Now, some five hundred years later—in our current era—the tide may be shifting once again. I do not want to be understood as equating the origin of cultural complexes with the geographical expansion and contraction of civilizations, but one can see 1492 as being a critical date for the beginning of the rise of the West and the beginning of the decline of Islam, and it is worth noting that the coincident interlocking of date and place did help shape the ripe conditions for the genesis of potent cultural complexes.

Figure 4.3 The rise of Islam to 750 CE.
(https://aras.org/vision-reality-complex)

The cultural complexes of Islam and the West

To say that the rise of the West is at the core of one cultural complex and that Islam is at the core of another is, of course, a gross oversimplification. For instance, there are multiple local and regional complexes that get caught up in these mega–cultural complexes. In the West, for instance, old French, German, English, and American rivalries and hatreds have been stirred up, just as in the Islamic world Sunni, Shiite, Kurdish, and other tribal feuds have been activated. And all of these cultural complexes—Western and Islamic—have been thrown together to form the conditions for a global "perfect storm" of colliding cultural complexes.

But, if we take 1492 as a turning point in defining the history of Islam and the history of the West and in giving rise to two very different kinds of cultural complexes, we can begin to sketch—only in the broadest of strokes because of space limitations—some of the characteristics of these cultural complexes.

On one hand, 1492 marks the beginning of the ascendancy of the New World with its "discovery" of the Americas. In addition to the New World providing just the right climate for the creation of a set of remarkable values such as democracy, freedom, and the sanctity of the individual, it has also given rise to a particular type of cultural complex characterized—especially in the United States and its relative "newness" on the world stage—by

*   Addiction to heroic achievement
*   Addiction to height
*   Addiction to speed
*   Addiction to youth, newness, and progress
*   Addiction to innocence[15]
*   And, most importantly, a profound belief in the resilience of the Western—and especially, the American—group spirit, which can easily translate itself into arrogance and grandiosity

On the other hand, 1492 also marks the beginning of the retreat of Islam from the West—and a long steady decline for the past five hundred years of Islam's ability to take creative initiative in the intellectual, economic, and social realms. This decline in Islamic power and influence has led to a cultural complex in the Islamic world and especially in its groups of radical fundamentalists that can be characterized by adherence to

- Purity
- Absolutism
- Tradition
- Incorruptibility

These first four characteristics of the cultural complex of Islamic fundamentalism are rather perfectly mirrored in their bipolar opposite, that is, the cultural complex of Christian fundamentalism in the United States. The next two features I want to highlight are more unique to the cultural complex of Islamic fundamentalism.

- Renunciation of materialism (as so awesomely symbolized and concretized by turning America's addiction to speed, height, and material success against itself in the attack on the World Trade Center).
- And, most importantly, a profound wound at the center of its group spirit that has given rise to despair and suicidal self-destructiveness. Repeated humiliation is at the heart of much of the Arab world's experience of itself and the fear of and rage at humiliation constitutes a most dangerous core symptom of the Islamic cultural complex. (For instance, Saddam Hussein's fall from power is seen by much of the Arab world as another Arab humiliation at the hands of the West rather than the collapse of a ruthless tyrant.)

If you mix all of these ingredients together, you will see that we have a truly horrific recipe for a witches' brew of cultural complexes that has mobilized huge energies in the life of nations and at the group level of the psyche in the individual, including most people reading this chapter. These aroused cultural complexes can activate what I have described elsewhere as the "archetypal defenses of the group spirit."[16]

Archetypal defenses of the group spirit

When a group has been attacked at the core of its being and values—as the United States was on 9/11—or when a group has been corroded at the core of its being and values—as Islam has been for the past five hundred years—I believe that archetypal defenses of the group spirit are mobilized to protect the vulnerable and injured group spirit, much in the same way that Donald Kalsched has postulated happens to the personal spirit of the traumatized individual.[17] These archetypal or *daimonic* defenses are ferocious and inhuman. The daemonic defenses often direct their primitive aggression back onto the wounded spirit of the group as evidenced in the self-mockery and self-denigration entrenched in the humor and self-perception of any number of oppressed minority groups. But, just as often, these same daimonic archetypal defenses of the group spirit can turn their savage aggression out onto whomever or whatever appears to be a threat to the spirit, basic value, or identity of the group. I see this response as automatic, reflexive, and in some ways the most natural way for the group psyche in the grips of a cultural complex to react. Those individuals who become the human embodiments of the "archetypal defenses of the group spirit" can torture people in prison. They can behead people. They can blow themselves and others up without regard to their own personal being or those who happen to be in their path. As defensive agents of a wounded group spirit, they are not constrained by normal human values or concerns. They are truly impersonal representatives of the group and its wounded spirit.

Considering the rise of radical Islamism in terms of the model of the archetypal defenses of the group spirit that I am proposing, Islamism and its terrorist agenda can be understood as an expression of this defensive pattern in an activated cultural complex. From this point of view, Bin Laden and the Mujahideen are *Daimones*—human but terrifyingly impersonal incarnations of archetypal defenses of the collective spirit. Their Islamist dream of creating a new "caliphate" can be interpreted as a geographic projection of a wish to restore a wounded collective Muslim spirit through the creation of an empire that transcends national boundaries—perhaps in their mind's eye looking a bit like the map of the Islamic world in 750 CE. The traumatized collective spirit of the Muslim world suffered centuries of humiliation at the hands of a rapidly expanding Western civilization that captured the scientific, technological, and materialistic initiative that once belonged to the Muslim world. But, by the most ironic of historical twists, the Muslim world—deeply wounded in its collective self-image—ended up with the richest share of the world's oil that is the current fuel for the materialistic advances of Western civilization. This is a perfect example of how cultural complexes beget cultural complexes.

The axis of evil

Bin Laden and al-Qaeda conceive themselves to be the avenging angels of the deeply and long traumatized spirit of the Muslim world—the specific trigger of their current vengeance apparently being the fact that infidel American troops remained in the holy lands of Saudi Arabia after the first Gulf War in 1991. The possession of one group by a cultural complex can automatically trigger its bipolar, reciprocal opposite in its rival, and so Islamist fundamentalists and their Western counterparts have been on a nightmarish merry-go-round. It is no accident that George Bush made a slip of the cultural unconscious when he first referred to a "crusade" as the US response to the World Trade Center and Pentagon bombings. Bush's slip was reflexive and automatic; it was backed up by a centuries-old memory. A crusade is our cultural complex's answer to a holy jihad.

For many in the West then, the Islamic fundamentalist terrorists have become the Daimones—what Bush called "the evil-doers." Bush painted a dramatic picture of these "evil-doers" literally linked together in a global "axis of evil" that includes Iraq, Iran, and North Korea. Simultaneously, for much of the Muslim world and many in the Western world as well, George Bush—like Bin Laden, self-appointed in his role—has also become an arch *Daimone*. And, it is precisely at this intersection—where the Daimones or archetypal defenses of the spirit of one group's cultural complex trigger the Daimones of another group's cultural complex—that I think we can more accurately locate a real "axis of evil"—be it the daimonic forces of Sharon aligned against the daimonic forces of Arafat, or the daimonic forces of Bush aligned against the daimonic forces of Osama bin Laden. These negative alignments truly form an axis in the sense that a direct line or connection is drawn between the Daimones of one group, protecting their sacred center, and the Daimones of a rival group, protecting their sacred center. Such negative alignments or axes create the conditions for the eruption of violence and wholesale destruction. Through the linking of the daimonic defenses in one group with the daimonic defenses of another, the cultural unconscious in multiple groups becomes ripe for the wholesale emergence of evil. Out of such potent negative alignments springs an "axis of evil" that is founded on the archetypal defense patterns of interlocking cultural complexes—for instance, of fundamental Islamism, of fundamental Christianity, and of fundamental Judaism.

As we see from the radical Islamist movement and the West's response (or, taken from the point of view of Islam, from the West's rise and the Islamist response to it), cultural complexes that trigger archetypal defenses of the group spirit tend to have long, repetitive histories. In terms of intergroup conflict, Christians, Jews, and Muslims have been at it for 1,200–2,000 years. Black and white people in America have been at it for over three hundred years. Freudians and Jungians have been at it for almost a hundred years. What makes the complexes that drive these conflicts so potent is that they take on a life of their own, not only in the group's response to attacks on its collective spirit, but also in the way that these complexes seem to take up permanent residence at the cultural level of the psyche in the individual members of their respective groups.

Conclusion

We hold up strange mirrors to ourselves and to one another when we start to explore cultural complexes as part of our individual and our group development. Our cultural complexes get all mixed up not only with our personal history and complexes but also with other cultural complexes as well. If we do not sort through our cultural as well as personal complexes carefully, we end up—at a minimum in the unconscious—feeling responsible for, identified with, or traumatized by events that belong to our cultural complexes far more than our personal complexes. Failure to consider cultural complexes as part of the work of individuation puts a tremendous burden on both the personal and archetypal realms of the psyche. Tremendous psychic energy in the individual and in the group can be bound up in unconscious cultural complexes and the inter- and intragroup conflicts that are their natural expression.

Conceptualizing intractable group conflicts (even those as large in scale as Islam and the West) in terms of cultural complexes allows us to make use of our one-hundred-year experience with complex theory. Most modestly, we have learned from our work with personal complexes that there is no quick fix or easy resolution to complexes; we are knowledgeable about the accumulation of stereotypical memory and behavior that accrues around any complex; and we are prepared for the seemingly endless autonomy and vexing unconsciousness of complexes. In speaking of the resolution of personal complexes, Jung warned, "A complex can be really overcome only if it is lived out to the full. In other words, if we are to develop further we have to draw to us and drink down to the very dregs what, because of our complexes, we have held at a distance."[18]

Applying that same wisdom to cultural complexes, we certainly have had recent experience in the Balkans, in the Middle East, and in any number of "hot spots" around the world about the need to drink "down to the very dregs" our cultural complexes. Formulating these phenomena in terms of cultural complexes is thus a heavy prescription, rather than a panacea; but it also allows us to appreciate and make more room for a level in the individual's psyche that belongs neither to personal experience nor to the archetypal depths and permits us a way to work toward deeper understanding of the role of cultural complexes in structuring the psychological responses of individuals and groups in the face of particular conflicts.

Even more importantly in my mind, the theory of cultural complexes and their archetypal defenses of the group spirit suggest that Jung was not entirely correct when he said, "Nowadays particularly, the world hangs by a thin thread, and that thread is the psyche of man."[19] An important piece was left out of that otherwise remarkable—one might even say—primal insight. The fate of the world does not, in fact, hinge on the thread of the individual psyche. Rather, the emergence of a theory of cultural complexes suggests that an understanding of the individual psyche through its consciousness will not be enough. The group itself will need to develop a consciousness of its cultural complexes. Perhaps each injured culture—be it Balkan, American, African American, White, Palestinian, Israeli, Iraqi, Catholic, Jewish, Jungian, Freudian, Men, Women (the list is endless once you begin to think in terms of cultural complexes)—needs to learn how to drink to the dregs its own complexes as well as those of its neighbors, allies, and enemies. To settle down the archetypal defenses of the group spirit, the collective psyche itself and its often traumatized, sometimes immature or stunted, spirit needs to individuate—and this is not the work of an individual alone or of analysis alone.

Notes

1 Copyright © 2006 John Wiley & Sons, Ltd. Thomas Singer, "The Cultural Complex: A Statement of the Theory and Its Application," *Psychotherapy and Politics International* 4 (2006): 197–212. doi:10.1002/ppi.110.

2 C. G. Jung, "Studies in Word Association" (1904–07/1910), *The Collected Works of C. G. Jung,* vol. 2, *Experimental Researches* (Princeton: Princeton University Press,1973).

3 C. G. Jung, "The Tavistock Lectures" (1935), *The Collected Works of C. G. Jung,* vol 18, *The Symbolic Life: Miscellaneous Writings* (Princeton: Princeton University Press, 1977), ¶149.

4 William McGuire, *Bollingen: An Adventure in Collecting the Past* (Princeton: Princeton University Press, 1989).

5 C. G. Jung, "Wotan" (1936), *The Collected Works of C. G. Jung,* vol. 10, *Civilization in Transition* (Princeton: Princeton University Press, 1970), 189–190.

6 C. G. Jung, *Memories, Dreams, Reflections,* ed. Aniela Jaffé (New York: Pantheon, 1963).

7 C. G. Jung, *Analytical Psychology: Notes of the Seminar Given in 1925,* ed. William McGuire (Princeton: Princeton University Press, 1989), 41–42.

8 Joseph Henderson, "The Cultural Unconscious," in *Shadow and Self* (Wilmette, IL: Chiron Publications, 1990), 102.

9 Joseph Henderson, *Cultural Attitudes in Psychological Perspective* (Toronto: Inner City Books, 1984).

10 Thomas Singer and Samuel Kimbles, eds., *The Cultural Complex: Contemporary Jungian Perspectives on Psyche and Society* (London and New York: Brunner Routledge, 2004).

11 Aryeh Maidenbaum, ed., *Jung and the Shadow of Anti-Semitism* (Berwick, ME: Nicolas-Hays, 2003); C. G. Jung, *Letters,* Vol. 1 (Princeton: Princeton University Press, 1973), 147–149.

12 John Perry, "Emotions and Object Relations," *Journal of Analytical Psychology* 15, no. 1 (1970): 1–12.

13 Jung, "Wotan," ¶395.

14 William H. McNeill, *The Rise of the West: A History of the Human Community* (Chicago and London: University of Chicago Press, 1963).

15 Micheal Gellert, *The Fate of America: An Inquiry into National Character* (Washington, DC: Brasseys, 2001).

16 Thomas Singer, "The Cultural Complex and Archetypal Defenses of the Collective Spirit: Baby Zeus, Elian Gonzales, Constantine's Sword, and Other Holy Wars," *The San Francisco Jung Institute Library Journal* 20, no. 4 (2002): 4–28; "Cultural Complexes and Archetypal Defenses of the Group Spirit," in *Terror, Violence and the Impulse to Destroy,* ed. John Beebe, 191–209 (Zurich: Daimon Verlag 2003).

17 Donald Kalsched, *The Inner World of Trauma: Archetypal Defenses of the Personal Spirit* (London and New York: Routledge, 1996).

18 C. G. Jung, "Psychological Aspects of the Mother Archetype" (1938/1954), *The Collected Works of C. G. Jung,* vol. 9i, *Archetypes and the Collective Unconscious* (Princeton: Princeton University Press, 1954/1959), ¶184.

19 William McGuire and R. F. C. Hull, *C. G. Jung Speaking* (Princeton: Princeton University Press, 1977), 303.

5   Playing the race card

A cultural complex in action

From *Sacral Revolutions: Reflecting on the Work of Andrew Samuels*, Routledge, 2010.[1]

As Barack Obama, a black man, battled Hillary Clinton for the Democratic nomination to run in the 2008 presidential election, my interest in cultural complexes took sharper, more specific focus as the issue of race inevitably surfaced in the heat of the primary competition. The cultural complex of race has been among the most virulently destructive and intractable complexes throughout the history of the United States, and the shape it took in the run up to the 2008 election was quite remarkable. How the race card was played in that election revealed an almost surgical anatomy of the workings of a cultural complex in terms of how the underlying emotional dynamics of the collective psyche can both be manipulated and shape the outcome of political processes.

Can we find a way to bring together passionate partisanship and psychological objectivity in a discourse on the forces that propel groups of people to align themselves into sharply differing positions on social, economic, and spiritual issues? Put another way—can we find a psychological attitude that allows us to talk about politics in a meaningful way that does not just give us license to be one more species of political "talking head," expressing endlessly biased political opinions in the name of a professional persona?

I do not pretend to have the answers to these difficult questions, but I would like to offer one psychological way of considering these matters that allows us to take into account the deep and unpredictable emotional currents in the group and individual psyche—unconscious as well as conscious— without too quickly identifying with one side or another in a polarizing conflict. I believe that the concept of the "cultural complex" is a notion that allows us to speak both to the passions of political conflict (and to one's own

Figure 5.1 Rene Cox's *Yo Mamas Last Supper:* A rather tricksterish playing of
        the race card, designed perhaps to trigger a cultural complex of white
        Christians.
(https://aras.org/vision-reality-complex)

subjective passion) and to a search for objectivity in understanding what
underlies specific political conflicts. The recently concluded Democratic
primaries and the various ways in which "the race card" (Figure 5.1) were
played illustrate how the cultural complex can be useful in shedding light on
the relationship between deeply conflicted emotional undercurrents of the
collective psyche and political process.

   Attitudes, behaviors, and emotions around race form one of the most
potent cultural complexes in the psyche of all Americans—white people,
black people, Asians, Latinos, and every hybrid in between. To get a vis-
ceral feel for what I mean by the cultural complex of race living in the
psyche of every American, consider Toni Morrison's description of the
spreading poison of racism from her novel *Beloved*:

   [Stamp] believed the undecipherable language clamoring around the
   house was the mumbling of the black and angry dead. Very few had
   died in bed ... and none that he knew of ... had lived a livable life. Even
   the educated colored: the long-school people, the doctors, the teachers,
   the paper-writers and businessmen had a hard row to hoe. In addition to
   having to use their heads to get ahead, they had the weight of the whole
   race sitting there. You needed two heads for that.
       Whitepeople believed that whatever the manners, under every dark
   skin was a jungle. Swift unnavigable waters, swinging screaming
   baboons, sleeping snakes, red gums ready for their sweet white blood.
   In a way, he thought, they were right. The more coloredpeople spent
   their strength trying to convince them how gentle they were, how clever
   and loving, how human, the more they used themselves up to persuade
   whites of something Negroes believed could not be questioned, the
   deeper and more tangled the jungle grew inside.
       But it wasn't the jungle blacks brought with them to this place from
   the other (livable) place. It was the jungle whitefolks planted in them.
   And it grew. It spread. In, through and after life, it spread, until it
   invaded the whites who had made it. Touched them every one. Changed
   and altered them. Made them bloody, silly, worse than even they wanted
   to be, so scared were they of the jungle they had made. The screaming
   baboon lived under their own white skin; the red gums were their own.[2]

The cultural complex of race with its mumbling voices of "the black and angry dead" and the "screaming baboon ... under their own white skin" became central voices in the Democratic primaries during the first half of 2008 and continued during the general election on the occasion of a black man becoming the nominee of the Democratic party for president of the United States for the first time in American history. Long simmering fear, rage, and hatred lurk just beneath the surface of the collective psyche on both sides of the nation's intractable racial divide.

The political landscape can be soiled instantaneously when the emotional and ideological toxins of the cultural complex of race are released into the environment by engaging in the time-honored political poker of "playing the race card." It takes very little for a politician to trigger the roiling emotions of the cultural complex of race. A single coded word or short phrase such as "white working-class Americans" can become a trigger for activating virulent emotions in what amounts to a word association test of the collective psyche.

> *Playing the race card* is an idiomatic phrase referring to an allegation raised against a person or group who has brought the issue of race or racism into a debate, perhaps to obfuscate the matter. ... It refers to someone exploiting prejudice against another race for political or some other advantage.[3]

In the language of the cultural complex, "playing the race" card detonates the landmine of one group's most powerful negative emotions and collective memories against another group's very existence.

I want to offer a brief synopsis of how "playing the race card" has come alive in the current 2008 presidential elections. Many different groups and subgroups have had different "cards" to play to achieve varying political purposes—but most are motivated by the desire to speak to and manipulate the powerful, nonrational affects of cultural complexes to get various groups to feel, think, and vote in one way or another based on the deep-seated feelings and memories of each particular group's experience. Race stirs up very primitive reactions that become more stereotypical the closer they get to the archetypal core of cultural complexes. This rough sketch of some of the cards that have been played reveals a cultural complex in action.

Card one: "The race card will not be played"

During all of 2007 Barack Obama framed his campaign's stance to the "race card" as not wanting to play it at all. He advocated a post-racial politics in which he insisted that the color of his skin should not be a primary issue in the campaign. He was attractive to many because he presented himself as a new generation of black leader for whom race was no longer the defining issue, and he offered a new way of being that transcended racial differences. That very post-racial posture, the refusal to play the race card as perhaps a new way to play the race card, made many black people suspicious of Obama for not being black enough. Black aides within his own campaign urged him to give his wife, Michelle, a more active role as a way of affirming his black identity. In view of what subsequently unfolded in the Democratic primaries, Obama's initial post-racial posture can be described as a good faith attempt to do an "end-run" on the cultural complex level of group experience.

Card two: "The race card will be played—but you played it first!"

Obama's post-racial politics worked quite well until his stunning victory in the January 5, 2008, Iowa caucus. In other words, it was not until Obama's candidacy became a real threat to the established Democratic and Republican leadership that race began to insert itself into the elections. This new phase of the race card game was inaugurated by Bill Clinton in late January 2008, when he suggested just prior to the South Carolina primary that Obama might win that state because of its large black vote. This was the first time race was overtly introduced into the Democratic primaries as a significant factor.

After Obama won South Carolina, Bill Clinton further compounded the race issue by seeming to dismiss Obama's victory by comparing it to Jesse Jackson's strong showing in the state in 1984 and 1988—basically saying that South Carolina is an easy state for a black candidate to win but it is of no broader significance. Clinton later went on to say that he was not the one to introduce the "race card" in South Carolina. He would claim that the Obama campaign had, in fact, stacked the deck so that any mention of race at all was going to be seen as "playing the race card" and that it was the Obama team that first played the race card.[4]

Card three: "The angry black preacher appears on Fox News"

In March 2008, an even more inflammatory racial card was introduced— not by the Clintons—but by the right-wing Fox News that uncovered and continuously played video tape of incendiary racial rhetoric from Obama's own minister, Reverend Jeremiah Wright. The "race card" now seemed to spring full blown from Obama's own religious community where Wright was shown accusing the United States government of infecting black people with the AIDs virus and welcoming the 9/11 attack as the "chickens coming home to roost"—that is, as punishment of the United States for its own international "terrorist" activity. The images of an angry black minister playing the "race card" was the very cultural complex "bomb" that both the Republicans and the Clintons had been hoping might come out of nowhere, explode, and cause Obama's apparently unstoppable momentum to implode. The irony is that it was Obama's close affiliation with Wright that handed his rivals the "race card" they had been waiting to play—and they didn't even have to play it themselves other than to show it endlessly on TV.[5]

Card four: The Trump card—"If the race card is going to be played, we are going to play it in a totally new way"

The Reverend Wright tapes ushered in another new phase in the "race card" poker game in which Obama had to modify his post-racial politics to include the realities of the divisiveness that festers in the deeply entrenched cultural complexes of both black and white people. Obama chose to energetically probe the emotional and psychic realities of the cultural complex of race in his Philadelphia speech of March 18, 2008. In the language of psychology, Obama chose to make the cultural complex itself more conscious rather than to project "its screaming baboons, sleeping snakes, and red gums" on to a rival group or to manipulate its potent affect to further intensify the fear and hate of one group for another.

Political expediency and Obama's own integrity demanded that he no longer do an "end-run" on race in his post-racial candidacy. In my mind, this was the moment when Obama truly emerged as presidential, because he showed his capacity to deal directly with a cultural complex in a psychologically insightful way. He chose to make the complex itself more conscious rather than to use the unconsciousness of the complex for his own purposes.

Using the criteria I have laid down elsewhere to define a cultural complex, let's look at elements of Obama's Philadelphia speech to see how he spoke to the complex in a psychological way that opened up the festering wound of race for dialogue rather than manipulating it to poison one part of the population against another.[6]

Obama began by locating the cultural complex of racial division within his own psyche, as well as the collective psyche of the nation as a whole:

> I am the son of a black man from Kenya and a white woman from Kansas. I was raised with the help of a white grandfather who survived

a Depression to serve in Patton's Army during World War II and a white grandmother who worked on a bomber assembly line at Fort Leavenworth while he was overseas. I've gone to some of the best schools in America and lived in one of the world's poorest nations. I am married to a black American who carries within her the blood of slaves and slaveowners—an inheritance we pass on to our two precious daughters. I have brothers, sisters, nieces, nephews, uncles and cousins, of every race and every hue, scattered across three continents, and for as long as I live, I will never forget that in no other country on Earth is my story even possible.[7]

After locating the cultural complex in his own experience and psyche, Obama then goes on to define how this has played out in the American collective psyche for centuries. I will link his descriptions and language to the criteria I have outlined for defining and identifying a cultural complex:

• A cultural complex expresses itself in powerful moods and repetitive behaviors—both in a group as a whole and in its individual members. Highly charged emotional or affective reactivity is the calling card of a cultural complex:

(A) legacy of defeat was passed on to future generations (of blacks)—those young men and increasingly young women who we see standing on street corners or languishing in our prisons, without hope or prospects for the future. ... For the men and women of Reverend Wright's generations, the memories of humiliation and doubt and fear have not gone away; nor has the anger and the bitterness of those years... In fact, a similar anger exists within segments of the white community. Most working and middle class white Americans don't feel that they have been particularly privileged by their race. ... They are anxious about their futures, and feel their dreams slipping away. So when they are told to bus their children to a school across town; when they hear that an African American is getting an advantage in landing a good job or a spot in a good college because of an injustice, they themselves never committed; when they're told that their fears about crime in urban neighborhoods are somehow prejudiced, resentment builds over time.[8]

• A cultural complex resists our most heroic efforts at consciousness and remains, for the most part, unconscious:

The fact is that the comments that have been made and the issues that have surfaced over the last few weeks reflect the complexities of race in this country that we've never really worked through—a part of our unions that we have yet to perfect. And if we walk away now, if we simply retreat into our respective corners, we will never be able to come together and solve challenges like health care, or education, or the need to find good jobs in America.[9]

- A cultural complex accumulates experiences that validate its point of view and creates a store house of self-affirming, ancestral memories:

    As William Faulkner once wrote, "The past isn't dead and buried. In fact, it isn't even past." We do not need to recite here the history of racial injustice in this country. But we do need to remind ourselves that so many of the disparities that exist in the African American community today can be directly traced to inequalities passed on from an earlier generation that suffered under the brutal legacy of slavery and Jim Crow.[10]

- Cultural complexes function in an involuntary, autonomous fashion and tend to affirm a simplistic point of view that replaces more everyday ambiguity and uncertainty with fixed, often self-righteous attitudes to the world:

    ... race is an issue that I believe this country cannot afford to ignore right now. We would be making the same mistake that Reverend Wright made in his offending sermons about America—to simplify and stereotype and amplify the negative to the point that it distorts reality.[11]

- Cultural complexes have archetypal cores; that is they express typically human attitudes and are rooted in primordial ideas about what is meaningful, making them very hard to resist, reflect on, and discriminate:

    The Declaration of Independence was stained by this nation's original sin of slavery, a question that divided the colonies and brought the convention to a stalemate until the founders chose to allow the slave trade to continue for at least twenty more years, and to leave any final resolution to future generations. ... I chose to run for the presidency at this moment in history because I believe deeply that we cannot solve the challenges of our time unless we solve them together—unless we perfect our union by understanding that we may have different stories, but we hold common hopes; that we may not look the same and we may not have come from the same place, but we all want to move in the same direction—towards a better future for our children and our grandchildren.[12]

Card five: "The angry black man won't go away"

Obama's Philadelphia speech was groundbreaking and went a long way toward quieting some of the racial concerns that surfaced in many groups until Reverend Wright caused a further uproar with an appearance at the National Press Club on April 28, 2008. Wright repeated some of his more inflammatory opinions in the Question and Answer session, which threatened to lethally embroil Obama's candidacy in its identification with Reverend Wright. As a result, Obama more definitively distanced himself from Wright, which, in turn, drew this "race card" reaction from Glen Ford in BlackAgendaReport.com who played the "race card" from a more militant black point of view:

> It was the masterful preacher and seasoned political creature Wright ... who forced Obama to choose in the push and pull of Black and white American worldviews. Obama was made to register his preference for the white racist version of truth over Rev. Wright's, whose rejection of Euro-American mythology reflects prevailing African American perceptions, past and present. Rev. Jeremiah Wright laid bare the contradictions of Obama's hopeless racial "neutrality."[13]

Card six: "The resentful white man won't go away"

In the meantime, the Clintons were becoming angrier and more frustrated as it became clear that Obama had strategically outflanked and out campaigned them in almost every way. Their only and last hope was twofold—to claim that it was, in fact, Obama who had played the race card and to further play the "race card" themselves by mobilizing the poor, hard-working white people of Appalachia (southern Ohio and all of Kentucky and West Virginia) to vote based on their racial fear and hatred of black people. The Clintons' goal was to convince the uncommitted superdelegates that because of the racism endemic in the white, less well-educated working class, Obama could not win in many parts of the country and, therefore, would do less well than Hillary Clinton in a general election. By the time the Democratic primaries had reached West Virginia and Kentucky in May 2008, it felt as though the political process had sunk to the very dregs of the 350-year-old deeply entrenched cultural complex and was pitting the "blacks" against "the poor white trash"—a condition that Bill and Hillary Clinton of Arkansas knew as well as any political poker players in the United States. It is in that context that Hillary Clinton introduced the following coded phrase about "hard-working white Americans" to stir up the most negative racial feelings in her timely playing of the race card:

> Senator Obama's support among working, hard-working Americans, white Americans, is weakening again ... whites in both states who have not completed college (are) supporting me. There's a pattern emerging here.[14]

Conclusion

The race cards I have outlined are just a few of the more notable ones that have been played in the last several months. The point of this brief outline of how they have been played is that the cultural complex of race in America is far too potent to have not become a major—if not the major—issue in the 2008 presidential election. The American psyche has hardly finished with its long history of racial conflict and, although post-racial politics are a worthy goal, they are not yet an emotional reality in the American collective conscious or unconscious. The Reverend Wright, Geraldine Ferraro, West Virginia, North Carolina, Fox News, the Clintons, and many, many others have made that abundantly clear. Retrospectively, there is no way that the cultural complex of race could not have raised its Medusa-like head during this campaign and threatened to turn to stone even the most modest hope for a change in racial politics. An end-run on the cultural complex of race will not bring our country's dream of a more perfect union into being.

At the same time, what is truly encouraging in the face of the monstrously resistant and regressive forces that playing the race card invariably mobilizes is how much Obama has already accomplished. The way in which he has personally carried in his being as well as in his words the polarizing opposites of black and white, the hateful demons of "screaming baboons, sleeping snakes, and red gums," suggests that Obama may be among those rare leaders who have the capacity to carry in their psyches the cultural complexes that usually divide groups into warring factions. Many are able to experience in him and through him a transcendent force that shows us as individuals, as groups, even as a nation, a way to digest and metabolize the bitter racial legacy that has threatened to destroy us throughout our history.

Notes

1 "Playing the Race Card: A Cultural Complex in Action," in *Sacral Revolutions: Reflecting on the Work of Andrew Samuels,* ed. Gottfried Heuer, 252–260 (London: Routledge, 2010). Reprinted with permission of the publisher.
2 Toni Morrison, *Beloved.* New York: Vintage, 1987), 234. Excerpt(s) from BELOVED by Toni Morrison, copyright © 1987 by Toni Morrison. Used by permission of Alfred A. Knopf, an imprint of the Knopf Doubleday Publishing Group, a division of Penguin Random House LLC. All rights reserved.
3 Wikipedia, s.v. "Race card," https://en.wikipedia.org/wiki/Race_card.
4 Glen Greenwald, *Salon,* January 27, 2008,www.salon.com/opinion/greenwald/2008/01/27/clinton/.

5 Brian Ross and Rehab El-Buri, "Obama's Pastor: God Damn America, U.S. to Blame for 9/11," *ABC News*, March 13, 2008, https://abcnews.go.com/Blotter/story?id=4443788. Dana Milbank, "Could Rev. Spell Doom for Obama?" *The Washington Post*, April 28, 2008. "Wright Says Criticism Is Attack on Black Church," National Press Club, www.washingtonpost.com/wp-dyn/content/video/2008/04/28/VI2008042801115.html?hpid=topnews.

6 Barack Obama, "Barack Obama's Speech on Race," *The New York Times*, March 18, 2008. www.nytimes.com/2008/03/18/us/politics/18text-obama.html.

7 Ibid.

8 Ibid.

9 Ibid.

10 Ibid.

11 Ibid.

12 Ibid.

13 Glen Ford, "Pop Goes the Race Neutral Campaign," *Black Agenda Report*, April 30, 2018.

14 Kathy Kiely and Jill Lawrence, "Clinton Makes Case for Wide Appeal," *USA Today*, May 2008.

6 Snapshots of the Obamacare cultural complex

From *Analysis and Activism: Social and Political Contributions of Jungian Psychology*, edited by Emilija Kiehl, Mark Saban, and Andrew Samuels, Routledge, 2016.[1]

The delivery of healthcare in the United States has been a lightning rod political issue for decades. The Clintons' handling of healthcare reform (see Chapter 1 in this book) was both their biggest promise and greatest failure. Barack Obama picked up the mantle of healthcare reform and carried it into his presidency in 2008. What was originally called the Affordable Care Act *became* Obamacare, *a trigger word for all the potent emotions and simplistic ideas that accrued around the cultural complex of the unending healthcare debate in the United States.*

The collective psyche and cultural complex

The notion of complexes forming subpersonalities as a central part of the way in which Jung thought about the psyche and its structure is familiar to many. The extension of Jung's complex theory into our tradition's thinking about social and political realities makes use of this idea of subpersonalities, or splinter parts of the psyche, as having an autonomous life of their own in the collective psyche of groups as well as in the psyches of a group's individual members. Cultural complexes are actually made up of bits and pieces of psyche from all the individuals who are drawn by the numinous power and energy of political, social, economic, and spiritual forces that can engulf those who share a specific time, space, and unique historical moment.

The Rumor, by the German artist A. Paul Weber in 1944 (Figure 6.1), illustrates how a sinister collective beast can be formed by the psyches of individuals who are sucked into the orbit of a cultural complex—becoming

Figure 6.1 A. Paul Weber, *The Rumor.*
(https://aras.org/vision-reality-complex)

its eyes, its ears, its thoughts, its emotions. I use images throughout this chapter as a way to imagine how these phenomena live in the collective psyche, which, at its deeper levels, is far less about differentiated thought and much more about affect, image, and instinct.

The splinter personalities that come to embody the conflicts of a culture start to look and feel in the media as if they are actual personalities in their own right. Obamacare has become just such a character and player in the American political psyche. The issue of how best to deliver health care has been on the national agenda in one form or another for almost a hundred years. I became actively involved in the discussion during Senator Bill Bradley's 2000 run for the Democratic presidential nomination. I served in a very minor role on Bradley's health care team, but in the process, I became more familiar with the crisis of medical care delivery. At that time, approximately 40 million Americans had no form of health care insurance whatsoever. By the time Barack Obama was elected President in 2008, this national scandal had increased to 50 million uninsured.

Obama promised—as had his predecessors without success—to deliver health care reform, and his Affordable Care Act was signed into law in March 2010. With an uncanny ability to change a law into a psychological cultural complex, the Republican opposition quickly renamed the Affordable Care Act, calling it *Obamacare,* and, with their own political genius, created an image with the Three Stooges and Obama as the Fourth Stooge, an image that spoke to the racism motivating large numbers of people (Figure 6.2). In doing so, it attracted all the loathing, frustration, fear, and distrust that lurks in the American cultural unconscious, dividing and paralyzing the national will in its ability to address the health care delivery crisis in a straightforward and realistic way.

Figure 6.2 Obama as the Fourth Stooge, an image that speaks to the racism motivating groups.
(https://aras.org/vision-reality-complex)

You may wonder why I started this chapter with a 1944 image from Germany, but a recent quote from a Republican official brings the visual association closer to home in terms of how Obamacare is perceived by many Americans—perhaps even a majority. The official said, "Democrats bragging about the number of mandatory sign-ups for Obamacare is like

Germans bragging about the number of mandatory sign-ups for 'train rides' for Jews in the 40s."[2] It is the emotional inflammation of the national psyche around Obamacare that makes this a subject worthy of psychological exploration. If we were to create a contemporary word association test of cultural complex trigger words in in the United States, *Obamacare* would be at the top of the list in its capacity to activate highly conflicted, powerful emotions that have truly possessed the American psyche.

I suggest visiting *Huffpost* and viewing the video "Anti-Obamacare Guest Has Meltdown on Live TV" (www.huffpost.com/entry/chris-hayes_0_n_5042261) to hear the not atypical exchange about Obamacare to get a feel for what I am writing about.[3] You don't have to pay attention to the specific arguments or so-called facts because they are not the point. The point is what happens to a discussion of complex issues when they get caught in a complex and its highly charged field of emotional reactivity.

Some facts about Obamacare

The number of medically uninsured Americans in 2010 was 49.9 million or 16.3 percent of the total population. In 2014, after Obamacare's shaky start, that number had decreased to about 41 million or 13.1 percent of the population; by 2015 the number had decreased to about 29 million or 9.1 percent; and by 2016 it had shrunk to 8.6 percent or 27 million uninsured. Democrats consider this a major achievement; Obamacare's critics portray it as the beginning of the end of the United States; and others of us view it as a small but significant improvement in an ongoing national disgrace.

As Tony Judt and many others have been telling us, the increasing discrepancy between the rich and the poor results in all sorts of social problems, including a decrease in the health of the population as a whole.[4] In their book *The Spirit Level: Why More Equal Societies Almost Always Do Better,* Richard Wilkinson and Kate Pickett include a graph that shows the relationship between income inequality and "ill health" (Figure 6.3)—the United States is almost off the charts among the industrialized nations of the world as having the poorest health as correlated with income inequality.

Figure 6.3 The relationship between income inequality and "ill health." (https://aras.org/vision-reality-complex)

Obamacare as a cultural complex

The problem of health care delivery has become exponentially more difficult to address because it has been hijacked and polluted by the potent affects and ideologies of the cultural unconscious in the form of a cultural complex. The fight over Obamacare continues to rage with Trump's administration trying to destroy it while promising better health care for all Americans.

Chester Arnold, a Northern California artist, has created an image suggestive to me of what a cultural complex looks and feels like—although that was certainly not his conscious intention (Figure 6.4). A cultural complex is made up of all sorts of random stuff, bit and pieces of psychic and material reality that come together in a potent ball that can repetitively roll over and through the psyche of individuals and groups with an unstoppable force—a kind of collective incarnation of the ancient Greek myth of Sisyphus who was condemned to roll a huge boulder up a hill that would eternally roll back down the hill and need to be pushed back up again and again.

Chester Arnold's captivating image reminds me of what I first learned about *teratomas* in medical school: the stuff of a cultural complex is sometimes as hideous and mixed up as a teratoma. These are tumors consisting of different types of tissue such as skin, hair, teeth, fingernails, and muscle, which are caused by the development of independent germ cells. Highly organized and totally chaotic tissue grow randomly together in an ugly mass that is unforgettable. Analogous to a teratoma, a cultural complex has bits and pieces of thought, image, memory, affect, and behavior that glom together in a mass that defies rationality but very powerfully influences, even takes over, the more everyday "tissue" of social reality that surrounds it. Once you have experienced a cultural complex in yourself or someone close to you, its reality and its influence are undeniable.

As in the painting by Chester Arnold (Figure 6.4), the Obamacare complex draws to itself every bit of flotsam and jetsam in the American psyche, preventing anything but the most primitive ideation and affect, dividing the country into Us versus Them polarities across which no bridges can be built. It is a Sisyphean ball that includes the American flag, the kitchen sink, and everything in between. It rolls over the population in a mind-numbing and dumbing-down assault on every reasonable human faculty. Rational dialogue is nonexistent; the emotional charge on the issue is extreme; the collective memory of various competing groups carefully selects its own stories and facts by which to tell the story, rendering discussions on the issue endlessly repetitive and appealing to the most basic, ongoing conflicted themes in American history. I have created a simple diagram to illustrate these ongoing conflicted themes in the American collective psyche and history, which have become the central ingredients in the Obamacare cultural complex (see Figure 6.5). This diagram illustrates how I use the cultural complex model—a truly Jungian theory—to frame the problem in a way that

Figure 6.4 Chester Arnold, *Thy Kingdom Come II*, 72" × 94", 1999. (Courtesy of the artist. In the collection of the DiRosa Preserve, Napa.)

(https://aras.org/vision-reality-complex)

addresses mythology, politics, and psychology and moves from personal to cultural to archetypal.

The Obamacare complex is a lightning rod that ignites just about every divisive issue in the American psyche. The following core issues are the fuel rods of the complex. There is a profound divide about the role of the individual and the role of the community in looking after the health and welfare of the citizens. This sometimes gets characterized as the tension between capitalism and socialism or communism. There is a profound divide about what it means to be free and what it means to be responsible as a citizen—those advocating freedom often championing the notion that every citizen should look after themselves and even act as laws unto themselves by carrying guns—with few responsibilities to the whole community. This gets characterized as the rights of the individual being impinged upon by the demands of the government, which is further projected at a group level onto the fight between the states and the federal government. There is a profound divide between the rich and the poor, with the poor being scorned as failures in their ability to provide for themselves. There is a profound

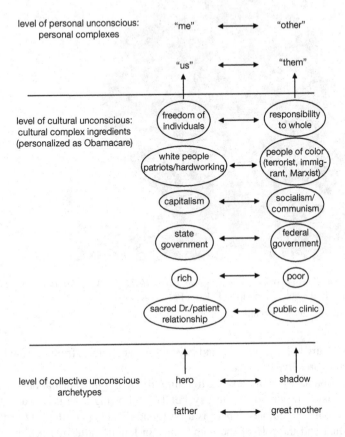

A Jungian Model of Unconscious "Us" vs. "Them" Dynamics
in the Formation of the Obamacare Cultural Complex

level of personal unconscious: "me" ⟷ "other"
personal complexes

"us" ⟷ "them"

level of cultural unconscious: freedom of ⟷ responsibility
cultural complex ingredients   individuals   to whole
(personalized as Obamacare)

white people ⟷ people of color
patriots/hardworking   (terrorist, immig-
rant, Marxist)

capitalism ⟷ socialism/
communism

state ⟷ federal
government   government

rich ⟷ poor

sacred Dr./patient ⟷ public clinic
relationship

level of collective unconscious   hero ⟷ shadow
archetypes

father ⟷ great mother

All of this can be turned upside down, depending on which group one
identifies with so that what is "us" becomes "them" and what is "me" becomes "other".

Figure 6.5 Diagram of the Obamacare cultural complex by Thomas Singer, MD.
(https://aras.org/vision-reality-complex)

racial divide between white people and people of color. There is a profound
divide along regional differences, between the coasts and the "heartland
of the country" and between the North and the South. All of this swirls
around in the cultural unconscious and fuels the Obamacare complex. At
the archetypal level, each side on the divide sees itself as being the "hero"

of the culture, wanting to save and protect what is of greatest value in the country. And each side sees its opposition as carrying everything shadowy and destructive in the country's history, acting as a curse on the nation's past, present, and future.

The telos of the Obamacare cultural complex

Jungian theory has it that there is an archetype at the core of every complex. It further posits that something of potentially positive value is locked up in the neurotic-seeming complex that has accrued around the nidus of the archetypal issue. This Aristotelian telos of a cultural complex, however, is often impossible to see, much less realize, in the fog of confusion and conflict that swirls around a culture's way of acting out one of its complexes. That is why the Chester Arnold painting is so true to the felt reality of a cultural complex—it collects more and more garbage that tends to roll over, dumb down, and numb all but the most fiercely persistent on either side of the conflict generated by the complex. Seeing through to the purposeful goal of the archetypal core of the Obamacare cultural complex is no easy task as the issues accruing around the core are all ferociously loaded with intense political energy, including rights of the individual, responsibility to the whole, the role of government, the divide between rich and poor, racial differences, the sanctity of doctor-patient relationships, the right to die, just to name a few. In this regard, John Beebe, who called my attention to the need to focus on the telos of the Obamacare cultural complex, reminded me that we might think of many of these themes as circulating around the controversial theory of Social Darwinism that Obama himself has cited as a core difference between Republicans and Democrats. For instance, in responding to a Republican budget proposal in 2012, Obama said the following: "It's nothing but thinly veiled Social Darwinism. It's antithetical to our entire history as a land of opportunity and upward mobility for everyone who's willing to work for it, a place where prosperity doesn't trickle down from the top, but grows outward from the heart of the middle class."[5]

Social Darwinism emerged in the late nineteenth century as an offshoot of Darwin's theory of evolution from which the concepts of natural selection and survival of the fittest were adopted by various groups as a scientific justification for their political, sociological, and economic philosophies. Those adopting Social Darwinism as their foundational value believe that "the strong should see their wealth and power increase while the weak should see their wealth and power decrease."[6] To those who embrace one form or another of Social Darwinism—whether they call it that or not or even know of the theory—the tenets of natural selection and survival of the fittest are embraced as if they are inviolable laws that govern the healthy development of societies as much as they govern the process of biological evolution. Of course, different movements make different claims as to which groups actually constitute the strong and the weak. Those who are economic Social Darwinists make the distinction about weak and poor based on economic success or failure. Those Social Darwinists who make the distinction between strong and weak on the basis of race, ethnicity, or gender will work covertly or overtly to ensure that the identified weaker group remains weak or gets even weaker—whether the group is black, Jewish, Palestinian, female, gay, white, Islamic, Christian, or whomever has been identified as weak.

The Social Darwinist vision of the human condition and destiny is tough and deterministic. That a threat to its thinking might be the "telos" at the archetypal core of the Obamacare debate is not what is clear to most and certainly not what one hears about in the day-to-day struggle over Obamacare's efficacy or value and the almost comedic way it is equated with the end of democracy. As John Beebe has written to me:

> The telos of the Obamacare complex is to force us to *look at* Social Darwinism in action, so as to make us see how inadequate that or any other theory might be when summoned to prevent a more deeply soul affirming inquiry into the issues that surround a matter as serious as how a society proposes to care for those of its citizens who fall ill.[7]

Nobody says outrightly, "Why should the strong, those who can afford healthcare in one way or another, bother about those who are poor and can find no way to afford healthcare coverage?" The fact is that the fundamental issue underlying the Obamacare debate, the way culture itself reacts to the Social Darwinist assumption, is what is at stake. The tricksterish telos of the complex, paradoxically, is to reveal the complex's fundamental absurdity. But this is not grasped by a nation whose energies are fully engaged in an unconscious debate about Social Darwinism. Instead, what we witness is the absurd lengths to which the unconscious devotees of Social Darwinism are willing to go to stop Obamacare. They display a level of *reductio ad absurdum* within the complex itself. Tragically, neither side on the debate can see that the cultural complex itself might be urging us, like in a dream in which we behave absurdly, to take a more critical look at our cultural thinking. And so the issues fester and are taken far more seriously than they deserve; all sides accumulate grievances, collect their respective memories, and make their same polarizing arguments over and over again. The archetypal pressure fueling the debate, our culture's deep wish to think and feel more consciously about what we do and do not owe each other, without a theory to preempt such an effort, is simply not made conscious. The telos of the complex, which is finally nothing other than cultural consciousness, rarely surfaces and even more rarely enters the discussion of the issues, which remain stalemated. Beebe puts it this way:

> The Obamacare debate should move our culture to see the degree to which, in the Economic Myth, we have managed to assume a Social Darwinist baseline as the given for how culture solves its most fundamental problems ... to see that, and to force us to realize, given the absurdity of some of the resulting debate, how narrow a base that really is.[8]

This does not mean we don't have the psychological, political, and human responsibility to make these unconscious dynamics of the cultural complex as conscious as possible. As the Obamacare example may suggest, our goal as Jungians might be to help reveal, with a healing irony, the telos of such cultural complexes and to look beneath their overt content with a psychological attitude at the purposive process of the complex itself. Let me put it another way: imagine what the discussion of Obamacare might be like if we substituted the African concept of Ubuntu, of the "interconnectedness of all human beings" for the Social Darwinist core of the cultural complex. Of course, the *reductio ad absurdum* vicious cycle would come full circle when those advocating a more Social Darwinist position about Obamacare might challenge my substituting the Ubuntu vision of human connectedness and say simply that I am caught in a cultural complex and refuse to look at the economic realities of delivering health care.

The Coelacanth and the primitive filtering system of the collective psyche

Cultural complexes are both highly specific to unique historical situations and, as structures of the group psyche, ubiquitous in human society. We have been exploring this theme of specificity and general applicability in volumes on Australia, *Placing Psyche;* on Latin America, *Listening to Latin America;* on Europe, *Europe's Many Souls,* and Far East Asia and the United States in two new volumes forthcoming from Routledge—*Spokes on the Wheel: Far East Asian Cultural Complexes* and *Cultural Complexes and the Soul of America*. I sometimes think of the collective psyche—both as it lives in the world and as it inhabits each individual—as being that part of the psyche/brain that filters what is happening in the world in a way that is analogous to the primitive kidneys that enabled the first amphibians such as the coelacanth to survive out of the water (Figure 6.6). Their kidneys

Figure 6.6 A coelacanth closely resembles the ancestral fish that first emerged
from the water to walk on land some 400 million years ago.
(https://aras.org/vision-reality-complex)

allowed these creatures to maintain an inland sea, even as they walked out
of the ocean. The kidney filters out what is toxic and retains what is essential for the survival of the organism. The evolution of the kidney, as opposed
to the Social Darwinist derivative of evolutionary theory, allowed human
beings to develop from our amphibian ancestors by allowing us to survive
on land while maintaining our individual inland sea. Today, humans also
swim in the sea of our collective human psyche, and we can think of cultural
complexes as the distillates of the collective psyche's rather crude filtering
function. I am quite certain that one day, something akin to what we call
cultural complexes will, when stimulated by cultural complex trigger words
such as *Obamacare,* light up in neuroimaging studies those parts of the
brain that link affect, memory, ideation, image, and behavior.

Notes

1 "Thomas Singer," Snapshots of the Obamacare Cultural Complex," in *Analysis
and Activism: Social and Political Contributions of Jungian Psychology*, edited by
Emilija Kiehl, Mark Saban, and Andrew Samuels, 147–156 (London: Routledge,
2016). Reprinted with the permission of the publisher.
2 Amanda Terkel, "Tennessee GOP State Senator Likens Obamacare Sign-Ups to
Nazi Death Trains," *HuffPost*, May 5, 2014, www.huffpost.com/entry/obamacare-
holocaust_n_5267120.
3 Catherine Taibi, "Anti-Obamacare Guest Has Meltdown on Live TV," *HuffPost*,
March 27, 2014, www.huffpost.com/entry/chris-hayes_0_n_5042261.
4 Richard Wilkinson and Kate Pickett, *The Spirit Level: Why More Equal Societies
Almost Always Do Better* (London: Allen Lane, 2009), 20.
5 Amie Parnes, "Obama: Paul Ryan's Budget 'Nothing But Thinly Veiled Social
Darwinism,' " *The Hill*, April 3, 2012, http://thehill.com/video/administration/
219731-obama-paul-ryans-budget-nothing-but-thinly-veiled-social-darwinism.
6 Wikipedia, s.v. "Social Darwinism," last updated December 19, 2019, http://
en.wikipedia.org/wiki/Social_Darwinism.
7 John Beebe, personal communication, 2015.
8 Ibid.

7 Extinction anxiety

Where the spirit of the depths meets the spirit of the times, or extinction anxiety and the yearning for annihilation

From *Rocket Man: Nuclear Madness and the Mind of Donald Trump*, edited by John Gartner and Steven Buser, Chiron, 2018.[1]

I was invited to present a paper at the third Analysis & Activism conference in Prague in 2017. Trump's presidency was careening from one chaotic misadventure to the next as awareness of the impending catastrophe of climate change grew. Global anxiety seemed to be escalating exponentially, and it occurred to me that our plight was different from that which gave rise to the concerns of the existentialists following World War II. For them, the universe seemed absurd. For us, the very survival of the planet was now seriously in doubt.

The purpose of this chapter is to introduce the term *extinction anxiety* as an apt clinical descriptor for a symptom that affects all of us. Apocalyptic fantasies are as old as time, but the term *extinction anxiety,* which originates in such fears, has not been used to describe the psychic state of individuals and groups that are either consciously or unconsciously gripped by the dread of extinction.

As we have learned from Freud, anxiety is a warning signal that danger is present and that overwhelming emotions may be felt, giving rise to unmanageable helplessness. We may perceive the danger as arising from internal or external sources in response to a variety of powerful unconscious fantasies.

I hypothesize that extinction anxiety is flooding the planet, although it frequently expresses itself in a displaced form of group or cultural anxiety rather than in the direct experience of the fear of extinction. It is timely for us to give a clinical name to *extinction anxiety* as a type of "warning signal that danger is present," whether originating in irrational fear or irrefutable objective evidence. In a recently published book *The Dangerous Case of Donald Trump*, Noam Chomsky writes quite simply: "There are two huge dangers that the human species face. We are in a situation where we need to decide whether the species survives in any decent form. One is the rising danger of nuclear war, which is quite serious, and the other is environmental catastrophe."[2]

We know of the dangers, but we have not named *extinction anxiety* as a source of worldwide psychic distress.

It may seem surprising that this term has not been introduced to describe this profound disturbance in the individual and collective psyche. When I first began to consider the term, I did a search and discovered that the only use of *extinction anxiety* is to denote the extinction of a symptom in a behaviorist model. In that model, the term is used to describe the attempt to "extinguish conditioned fear." When I use the term *extinction anxiety*, I am not talking about the extinction of fear; I am talking about the *fear of extinction*.

Perhaps the closest we have come in the history of our profession to naming such anxiety is *existential anxiety*. Existential anxiety, born out of the disillusioning and dismembering experiences of World War I, the Great Depression, and World War II, convinced many that the universe was absurd and meaningless. "Existence precedes essence" was a way of saying that life did not come into being with a preexisting meaning but that meaning or "essence" had to be created out of one's own being. Finding oneself in a meaningless universe is not the same as facing the extinction of life as we know it. In other words, existential anxiety and extinction anxiety emerge out of different fears, although both are profoundly disorienting in the sense that we have lost our "place" in a world that had given us meaning with a feeling of relative safety. *Extinction anxiety* as part of the "spirit of our times" is different from the "spirit of the times" that gave rise to existential anxiety.

I am not writing this chapter to prophesize the end of times. Rather, my purpose in writing this chapter is to say that the intense, contemporary anxiety about the approaching end of time is real and needs to be taken with the utmost seriousness. Although extinction anxiety finds a voice in the direct expression of environmental groups and those concerned about nuclear war (see the recent letter signed by 16,000 scientists[3]), it finds less direct expression in other groups and individuals who are in fear of their own annihilation but who do not consciously link their deeply felt precarious status to the fear of the extinction of the world.

Appropriately enough, the term *extinction anxiety* literally popped into mind when I was working on a paper about Donald Trump. I was thinking about all the diverse groups around the world who fear that their unique identities and very existence are threatened: white people, black people, women, men, Latinos, Jews, Muslims, LBGTs, 60 million refugees around the globe, just to list a few of the groups in the grips of fear for their own survival. Could it be that they are all tapping into a deeper underlying extinction anxiety, which is the collective psyche's equivalent of the anxiety about death in the individual? I believe that extinction anxiety acts as a psychic radioactive background in our global society and that it fuels many of our concerns. For instance, climate change deniers on the right in the United States may be seen as denying the very real possibility of the planet's destruction as a way of defending themselves against the fear of extinction. Aligning himself with this attitude, Trump offers to staunch *extinction anxiety* by denying it is real and appointing a well-known climate change denier as his energy adviser. As we know, denial—whether at the individual or group level—is the most primitive defense in the psyche's arsenal of defenses to protect itself.

I believe that C. G. Jung was right in suggesting that the psyche has multiple layers that go down or up or around the individual to the family, to the clan, to the nation, to larger groups such as European or Asian, and even to primate and animal ancestors, finally finding its source in what Jung called the "central fire" (as illustrated previously in Figure 4.1).

We know that there are fault lines at every level of our global society. These fault lines that demarcate divisions between groups of people and nations run deep along tribal, national, religious, racial, and ethnic lines— perhaps all the way down to the central fire—the very core of psychic life itself. Today, I want to go straight down to the "central fire" because my thesis is that there is an anxiety that is emerging from that deepest level of the psyche through fault lines or channels that run back and forth from the very bottom of psychic life on the planet all the way up to the individual. We can imagine that extinction anxiety courses up and down along these channels as the carrier of the signal of alarm and great danger.

We can also imagine that along these fault lines, extinction anxiety is where the spirit of the times and the spirit of the depths meet. To tease out the idea that the spirit of the depths and the spirit of the times merge with one another in the phenomenon of extinction anxiety, I want to spend a few minutes circling around these two spirits in relation to extinction anxiety.

The spirit of the depths and extinction anxiety

"The spirit of the depths" refers to ancient and recurring themes of deepest concern to human beings: themes of death and rebirth, of meaning and meaninglessness, of suffering and joy, of loss and repair, of what is fleeting and what is eternal. From the "spirit of the depths" humankind has been experiencing apocalyptic fantasies since the dawn of human history. *Zarathustra;* from the

Bible, the Book of Daniel and Book of Revelations—all are steeped in the apocalyptic vision of the end of time.[4]

Perhaps the most moving modern expression of this vision from the spirit of the depths is William Butler Yeats' "The Second Coming," originally written in 1919 at the end of World War I:

> *The Second Coming*
> Turning and turning in the widening gyre
> The falcon cannot hear the falconer;
> Things fall apart; the centre cannot hold;
> Mere anarchy is loosed upon the world,
> The blood-dimmed tide is loosed, and everywhere
> The ceremony of innocence is drowned;
> The best lack all conviction, while the worst
> Are full of passionate intensity.
> Surely some revelation is at hand;
> Surely the Second Coming is at hand.
> The Second Coming! Hardly are those words out
> When a vast image out of *Spiritus Mundi*
> Troubles my sight: a waste of desert sand;
> A shape with lion body and the head of a man,
> A gaze blank and pitiless as the sun,
> Is moving its slow thighs, while all about it
> Wind shadows of the indignant desert birds.
> The darkness drops again; but now I know
> That twenty centuries of stony sleep
> Were vexed to nightmare by a rocking cradle,
> And what rough beast, its hour come round at last,
> Slouches towards Bethlehem to be born?[5]

Figure 7.1 can be viewed as a haunting image of that "rough beast," which has both a lion's body and a man's head. Figure 7.2 is a Trumpian parody of that "rough beast," which features a "gaze blank and pitiless as the sun."

Apocalyptic fantasy from the spirit of the depths is alive and well in the longing of Christian fundamentalists for the end of times in the rapture at Armageddon. And it has been alive and well in Isis and its Islamic apocalyptic vision of the end of times in the yearning to create the caliphate. These fantasies can be thought of as emerging from the depths of "the central fire" that gives birth to human psyche. We can also imagine, along with the Hindus, that the "central fire" can do just the opposite and take back into itself all of life and psyche, as in Vishnu's reabsorption into himself of the whole of the created cosmos.

Figure 7.1 The beast in Yeats' "The Second Coming."
(https://aras.org/vision-reality-complex)

Figure 7.2 Trump with a lion's body: The Rapture Is Imminent!
(https://aras.org/vision-reality-complex)

The "spirit of the times" and extinction anxiety

Our "spirit of the times" remains anchored mostly in the scientific mind, which has become wedded to technology and materialist consumerism. It is no accident that the Bulletin of Atomic Scientists has created and maintained a Doomsday Clock (Figure 7.3) since the dawn of the nuclear age in 1947 when the clock was set at seven minutes to midnight. Midnight marks the extinction of the human race.[6] Since its inception, the clock has fluctuated in predicting how much time we have left. In 1953, it was moved up to two minutes to midnight when both the United States and the Soviet Union exploded hydrogen bombs. It drifted back to three minutes to midnight until the election of Donald Trump when it was set closer to doomsday—two-and-a-half minutes to midnight.

Figure 7.3 The Doomsday Clock pictured at its most recent setting of "two and half minutes to midnight."
(https://aras.org/vision-reality-complex)

In the "spirit of the times," our extinction anxiety is fueled by undeniable objective evidence that life on the planet is seriously endangered. We know, for instance, that we have already entered the "sixth mass extinction event" in which it is predicted that one-half of the world's land and marine species could disappear by 2100 unless there is some other annihilating or transforming event that precedes the "natural unfolding" of the sixth mass extinction event.[7] As human beings, we are instinctually and archetypally connected with all life. The threat of the loss of all these nonhuman species contributes to extinction anxiety.[8]

What if the human psyche carries within it the deep memory of biological and geological evolution, that our evolutionary heritage is mapped in the brain? In what scientists call *deep time,* the Earth has experienced five mass extinctions. Four of these were triggered by climate change and were followed by large-scale reorganizations in the biosphere, opening gateways that ultimately led to the evolution of the human species. Does the "deep psyche" have a memory of "deep time" and these previous extinctions as reflected in the Hindu religious imagination? It is interesting to contemplate how this might be manifesting in our current spirit of the times.

More immediately, on a day-to-day basis, we are flooded with news of devastating fires, massive storms, terrorist attacks, and random mass killings. All of this heightens the horrifying fear that something is terribly amiss in the world. We are being flooded not only with way too much information and the staggering explosion of the global population, but also perhaps with too much interconnectivity. Imagine for a moment that everyone you see walking down the street or sitting in a coffee house communicating on their cellphone or computer is actually sending out billions of the same daily latent message: "It hasn't happened yet." What if our frantic interconnectivity is a global SOS expression of extinction anxiety? What if we are desperately clinging to one another in an effort to reassure ourselves we are not on a sinking or exploding ship?

I hope it has become clearer how I imagine extinction anxiety flowing up and down the layers of the ancient and contemporary global psyche that includes evolutionary time circulating in an accelerating negative feedback loop, up from the spirit of the depths to the spirit of the times and back "down" again, in which guns, storms, and nuclear threats merge with old and new apocalyptic visions.

The obvious next question is—so what? What can we do with this? Does it help to make conscious the unconscious extinction anxiety that is fortified today by the very real scarcity that stalks much of the world's population and that pits all sorts of groups against one another in the most intractable conflicts? I wonder if increased consciousness and political activism based on the awareness of global extinction anxiety offers some slim hope of humankind being able to make informed choices?

Conclusion

If extinction anxiety is sounding an alarm on behalf of the whole of creation where the spirit of the depths and the spirit of the times meet at every level of human experience then our response needs to come from the whole of the psyche in harnessing all of our political, psychological, and spiritual efforts to forge a unity of deep action on behalf of creation and against that which would destroy it. This may well require the extinction of our current worldview, which is focused almost exclusively on materialist reductionisms of all kinds.

No one has more vividly conveyed what is at stake than Cormac McCarthy in his strangely intimate post-apocalyptic novel *The Road*, which has created for me a parallel universe along whose devastated and dangerous road I often find myself walking in reverie.[9] I find myself in a world without electricity, cars, hot water, enough food, and the constant threat of murderous human beings who have lost all their humanity. In the mood of that reverie, I debate whether or not to buy a gun to protect my family—but we Americans already have more guns than people, some 350 million of them, and they don't seem to be protecting us from anything. Surely the wish to own a gun is an instinctive response to defend oneself in the face of heightened extinction anxiety. This is what extinction anxiety does to us!

Notes

1 Thomas Singer, "Extinction Anxiety: Where the Spirit of the Depths Meets the Spirit of the Times, or Extinction Anxiety and the Yearning for Annihilation," in *Rocket Man: Nuclear Madness and the Mind of Donald Trump,* edited by John Gartner and Steven Buser, 205–212 (Asheville, NC: Chiron, 2018). Reprinted by permission of Chiron Publications.

2 Brandy X. Lee, *The Dangerous Case of Donald Trump* (New York: Thomas Dunne Books, St. Martin's Press, 2017), 357.

3 Christensen, Jen "16,000 Scientists Sign Dire Warning to Humanity over Health of Planet," CNN, November 15, 2017, www.cnn.com/2017/11/14/health/scientists-warn-humanity/index.html.

4 For this section, I am indebted to Richard Stein, MD, whose "Living on the Edge of the Apocalypse: What Isis, The Christian Right, and Climate Change Deniers Have in Common" appears in The San Francisco Jung Institute Presidential Papers of 2016: https://aras.org/newsletters/aras-connections-special-edition-2016-presidency-papers.

5 William Butler Yeats, "The Second Coming," *Michael Robartes and the Dancer* (Churchtown, Dundrum: Cuala Press, 1921), 19–20. Available on the Internet Archive, https://archive.org/details/robertes00wby/page/n23.

6 Bulletin of the Atomic Scientists, Doomsday Clock, https://thebulletin.org/timeline.

7 Elizabeth Kolbert, *The Sixth Extinction* (New York: Henry Holt and Company, 2014).

8 I am indebted to Jeffrey Kiehl for personal communications about the section on "mass extinction events."

9 Cormac McCarthy, *The Road* (New York: Alfred A. Knopf, 2006).

Index

Note: Page numbers in *italics* indicate figures on the corresponding pages.

Printed in the United States
by Baker & Taylor Publisher Services